"Dogs are our link to paradise. They don't know evil or jealousy or discontent. To sit with a dog on a hillside on a glorious afternoon is to be back in Eden, where doing nothing was not boring — it was peace."

Milan Kundera
(The Unbearable Lightness of Being)

NEV GREEN
& MARK STIBBE

DO DOGS
GO TO
HEAVEN?

A Conversation

BOOKLAB

Copyright © Nev Green and Mark Stibbe
First published 2022 by Bella Books UK, a Paw Print/Imprint of BookLab
www.thebooklab.co.uk

25 24 23 22   7 6 5 4 3 2 1

British Library Cataloguing in Publication Data
A catalogue record for this book is available from the British Library.

ISBN 978-1-3999-3782-5

Cover design by Esther Kotecha

Printed in the UK

Contents

Introduction   7

Chapter 1:   Sophie R.I.P.   13

Chapter 2:   On Tears   15

Chapter 3:   Canine Empathy   19

Chapter 4:   A Load of Bull   23

Chapter 5:   Luther's Pup   27

Chapter 6:   My Master   31

Chapter 7:   In The Garden   35

Chapter 8:   True Friends   39

Chapter 9:   Heal/Heel!   43

Chapter 10:   Perfection   47

Chapter 11:   Chester's Dream   53

Chapter 12:   After Life   59

Chapter 13:   Shady Lands   65

Chapter 14:   In Memory of Tish   71

Chapter 15:   Consolation   75

Chapter 16:   Vegetarian Lions   81

Chapter 17:   Beam Me Up   87

Chapter 18:   Joy Bringers   93

Chapter 19:   The Very Dear One   99

Chapter 20:   A Fishy Heaven   105

Chapter 21: Molly's Tale   111

Chapter 22: A Dog Called Sprout   117

Chapter 23: A Wagging Tail   123

Chapter 24: Foxie and Pepper   129

Chapter 25: Argos – Not The Store   135

Chapter 26: Summerland   141

Chapter 27: All Things New   145

Chapter 28: When In Rome   151

Chapter 29: Original Sin   157

Chapter 30: Rainbow Bridge   161

Chapter 31: A Man's Best Friend   167

Chapter 32: Number One   175

Chapter 33: True Desperation   181

Chapter 34: My Master's Face   187

Chapter 35: Anima, Animal   193

Chapter 36: Dibley's Praise   199

Chapter 37: Our Final World   205

Chapter 38: Rest in Peace   211

Chapter 39: Beautiful Joe   215

Chapter 40: An Enchanted Place   217

Introduction

The date is September 8th 2022 and the world has just heard the news of the death of Queen Elizabeth II who has reigned over the United Kingdom and the Commonwealth for seventy years. During that time, two constant qualities have been her Christian faith and her love for her dogs. The Queen's favourite dogs were royal Corgis from Pembrokeshire. She loved them as a child. In the years after her coronation, she owned over thirty of them. One, Holly, made a cameo appearance at the beginning of the 2012 Olympics to help escort Daniel Craig (the actor who played James Bond) into the Queen's presence. Five years before she died, the Queen stopped breeding her own Corgis so that there would be none to mourn her after she had gone. Her final Corgi, named Willow, died in 2018. When people in the UK think of the Queen, which we are doing a great deal right now, we think of her either with her beloved dogs, or with her equally beloved horses.

There are many stories about the Queen's love of dogs, but one stands out for its insight into her empathy not only for dogs but also human beings. David Nott had been a surgeon in Aleppo and witnessed the most traumatic atrocities and injuries. He wrote a memoir about his experiences entitled *War Doctor,* subtitled, 'Surgery on the Front Line.' Published by Picador in 2020, it deservedly became a bestseller. Perhaps one of the most poignant moments he describes is the occasion when he met the Queen. Still carrying trauma in his body, he was ushered into her presence. Straightaway, and for no discernible reason known to him, David felt something give. The dam he had built to keep his emotions at bay began to crumble. He was on the point of releasing a great flood of tears. As David wrote, "Perhaps it is because she is the mother of the nation and I had lost my own mother."

The Queen, sensing David's distress, reached out and touched his hand. She then turned to a silver box. There were biscuits inside. "These are for the dogs," she said. She broke one in half and gave one half to David. They fed the Corgis under the table, and for the rest of their time together the Queen avoided all talk of Aleppo, choosing instead to chat about her dogs – how many she had, what their names were, their ages. As David stroked and petted them, all the distress began to ebb away, and he relaxed.

"There," said the Queen as they finished. "That's so much better than talking, isn't it?"

What a beautiful anecdote that is.

And how appropriate for a book like ours!

We believe with all our hearts that dogs have been put on this earth for a purpose. One of those purposes – as is vividly demonstrated in this royal tale – is for our healing.

But there are so many others besides.

Grief is in the air right now, so it seems appropriate that our book has arisen out of grief, the grief of losing a much-loved dog – Sophie, a 15-year-old Border Collie. Her passing was the catalyst for a long conversation between two grown men who are unashamed of their deep devotion to their canine companions, and who have had one big question they wanted to try and answer: where is Sophie now? Or, put another way, do dogs go to heaven? What you are about to read is not carefully structured; as Ann Hood has said, "Grief doesn't have a plot. It isn't smooth. There is no beginning and middle and end." It is not cerebral either; although we do tackle issues of faith and philosophy, in the end neither of us is reluctant to show our emotions. Men can build dams, as David Nott's testimony shows, but when it comes to our canine friends, all our defences disappear. We have both seen the toughest fellows fall apart when their dogs die.

We are also entirely unashamed of enlisting our very personal experiences of God – especially of his fatherly love and kindness – in trying to answer the question posed in the title of this book. To some we won't be explicit, dogmatic, theologically sound, or even righteous enough in what we say. To others we will seem perhaps a little too religious. To those of you who might be vexed by either of these extremes, we simply ask that you read our conversation as . . . well . . . just that – a conversation; a conversation between two old friends who are more interested in getting to the truth through telling stories and shedding tears than in sparring over theological issues and showcasing their intellectual prowess. Our aim all along has been to console each other by looking up beyond this earthly realm of trials into a layer of existence where the perfect Father wipes away every tear from our eyes. As Thomas Moore once said, "earth has no sorrow that heaven cannot heal." With all our hearts, we both believe it.

It has been said that Britain is a nation of dog lovers. If that is true, and the evidence supports it, then many millions of us have gone through the unspeakable pain of saying goodbye to a dog who has given us throughout its life a glimpse of unconditional love. This book is for all of you who have been through this trauma, or who have yet to face this dreadful day. We want you to know that there really is what many call a Rainbow Bridge where the dogs who have walked with us throughout the years wait until the moment of our own passing. When they see us wandering towards this crossing, they bound towards us, eager for a reunion whose depth of feeling would be a challenge for even the greatest poets to depict. When that ecstasy is over, both walk across that multi-hued, prismatic bridge into the realm where there is no more pain, no more dying, no more sighs, and no more crying.

In saying this, of course, we have already revealed the answer to the question posed by our book! But that's okay. We know it sounds like a well-worn cliché, but this conversation really isn't so much about the destination; it's about the journey. The blessings and the benefits aren't so much in our resounding answer as they are in the stories we tell and the insights we discover on the way. We hope that as you walk with us, you will find great consolation in the words that poured out of both of us as we wrote to each other.

As you prepare to read on, maybe you too have been remembering the Queen and her dogs. Maybe, like us, you have reflected how fitting it is that a nation of dog lovers has been ruled by one who perhaps doted on her canine companions more than any of us. There was, after all, even a Corgi room in Buckingham Palace where the dog beds were raised just above the ground so they wouldn't be disturbed by any drafts. I know many of us go to lengths that some would find indulgent, but that is perhaps another level, quite literally.

The Queen loved her dogs. As she has passed from this earthly realm today, maybe her dogs have been waiting in some celestial meadow, turning their heads with bright eyes towards the sight of an old woman in a hat shuffling with a walking stick, heading with stoic determination towards a bridge. Maybe they have run to her too, jumping towards her outstretched hand, wagging their tails at the sound of her much-missed chuckling.

If you feel that all this is too sentimental and speculative, maybe this book isn't for you.

And maybe, too, you missed it.

As the news of the Queen's death broke, something appeared in the grim grey skies above Buckingham Palace.

A lush and radiant rainbow.
Not one, in fact.
But two!
A glorious double rainbow.
Charting a course across the heavens.
Like a bridge.

Mark and Nev
September 8th 2022

1

Sophie R.I.P.

Dear Nev,

I'm so sorry to hear about Sophie. You must be heartbroken. I was always so impressed by her, and by your mutual devotion. Sophie was the most loyal and loving friend to you for so many years. She had such a calm and good nature. What a lovely soul she was. I'm so very sad for you that she's gone, though comforted by a holy thought I had many years ago, that the first ones to greet us on entering heaven's gates will be the dogs we loved and lost. God knows that for people like you and me this would be the ultimate reassurance that we are in the right and happiest place of all.

Lots of love my old pal,

Mark.

Dear Mark,

Thank you so much for your email; it means the most from those who truly understand.

Like you, I am convinced that we will meet again. When Chester died (my dog before Sophie), I had the most vivid dream of meeting him in a reception room as I entered heaven, and I knew then that this was so much more than just wishful thinking: it was one of *those* dreams.

As I prayed over the loss of Sophie, my Heavenly Father showed me that I was the very last thing she could smell, she could feel, and of which she was aware.

I know that would have been all she would have wished for.

Thank you again my friend – it means so much.

Love,

Nev.

2

On Tears

Dear Nev,

I was brought to tears by your dream about Chester and your description of your beloved Sophie's final moments. I was brought up to believe that big boys don't cry. It was part of the stiff-upper-lip culture of boarding school. I spent over fifty years trying to break it. Although this toxic belief had a lot of power over me, there were moments when its strong hold over me was loosened.

When I lost my first dog, my Black Labrador called Mijbil – Mij for short (named after the otter in *Ring of Bright Water*) – I was a vicar in Sheffield. I took her to the vet when it became clear that she was living in deep pain, beyond all hope of recovery. I sat on the cold consulting room floor after she was injected and held my tears until she had gone. I didn't want her to know I was upset.

Then, when I knew it was over, I looked up and howled. A primal reaction, I know. I can't explain it. I sobbed into the jaded mane around her neck. Tore myself away. Wandered out into reception, dog collar on (why I was wearing it, I'll never know), too traumatized to speak. Somehow I paid the bill – clinical, isn't it? Then I wandered out into the wintery streets, trying to stem the tears.

I have often reflected on this moment, though never spoken about it before, except to Cherith. I felt at the time, and still do, that this is the depth of empathy in the heart of God over our sufferings. While we have no answer to the question *why* (let's be honest about it; we won't know until the end), we do have an answer to the question *where*. God is with us in our trauma. Holding us too. Weeping.

That's enough for now. I need to recover.

Love,

Mark.

Dear Mark,

On tears: St Isaac the Syrian said, "When you reach the place of tears, then know that your spirit has come out from the prison of this world and has set its foot upon the path which leads towards the New Age. Your spirit begins at this moment to breathe the wonderful air which is there, and it starts to shed tears."

Since leaving my career in the police – in my day, very much the domain of the 'strong man' – I have had an ever-increasing tendency to shed tears, particularly in worship or when I am tangibly aware of the presence of God. You may remember a dinner we had together, when I tried to explain, with great difficulty, what I had experienced in C.S. Lewis's bedroom, as the tears were flowing. In his chapter on 'God as Spirit' in *The Orthodox Way*, the late Bishop Kallistos Ware refers to the *gift of tears* and likens it to the 'letting go' of speaking in tongues – "the crucial moment in the breaking down of our sinful self-trust and its replacement by a willingness to allow God to act within us." For me, speaking in tongues is rare; tears are frequent.

I identify with all that you recount of your emotions on the day that you lost Mij. In Sophie's case, I managed to make it home before I, too, howled as I collapsed in my chair and sobbed. The howl, I think, is an expression of pain and despair. But why such pain and despair? The only way that I could explain the sense of loss to my wife Lesley was that it feels I have lost part of *me*. Something of who I am, what makes me 'me', has gone. Part of that is the constant companionship. I could not, with any other person, spend the amount of time every day that I spent with Sophie by my side or at my feet. Even those we love the most would start to irritate with that kind of constant proximity. But not our dogs. They are not *another* but an extension of ourselves. However, it is more than just the physical companionship – in a bizarre way, I was convinced that Sophie (and Chester before her) thought like me, loved as I loved, and was always 'on my side.'

I wonder, does this reflect something of the nature of our relationship with Jesus? He is more than *another* – or, rather, we are more to Him than *another*. I in Him and He in me (John 17). In a strange and yet comforting way, I can grasp something more of what this means from the gift that Sophie has been to me.

This is helping.

Love,

Nev.

3

Canine Empathy

Dear Nev,

I love the St Isaac quote, which I didn't know, and the idea of a person's *spirit* shedding tears. Thank you for that; it's treasure. I remember well your tears after we visited C.S. Lewis's home. The older I get, what passes for my prayer life is less about words and more about sighing and crying. I think our howling at the death of our dogs is something similar – a prayer of protest, an incoherent lament. I don't know, really. One day I'm sure we will. Things in this world are not as they should be.

To expand on your powerful words about Sophie's incomparable companionship, about her being always at and on your side, I can relate to this. I also wonder if it's "a deeper magic still," to quote Lewis. When I was struck down with a very severe case of Bell's Palsy in 2015, I remember visiting my GP. When I came out, I was sporting a new eyepatch (like a pirate) and carrying steroids. The entire right side of my face was lopsided and disfigured.

Cherith was waiting for me in the car, with Bella – our Black Lab – behind her on the back seat. When I sat down in the front, Cherith could see that I was upset and reached over to hold my arm. At that point, the burden of the previous three impossible years, combined with this blow to my health, overwhelmed me and the tears began to fall.

Bella reached forward from behind me, closing the gap, and just leaned her chin very gently on my shoulder. That's all. It may seem like nothing to some – although not to you – but to me it was everything. I felt this tremendous reassurance and peace, that in the words of St Julian, "all shall be well, and all manner of thing shall be well."

And eventually it was.

I sometimes wonder if one of the reasons we feel the unique bond we do with our dogs is because they have this capacity – one that I think is more to do with the mystic than the zoologist – of transmitting a particular kind of empathy, one that brings a hint of what is promised to us in the Bible, that God is close to the broken hearted.

In other words, I wonder if the love of a dog is a merciful hint, within the natural order, of the love of God.

Maybe that's the *deeper magic still*.

Take good care of yourself.

Love,

Mark.

Dear Mark,

From *Timmy's in the well: Empathy and Prosocial Helping in Dogs,* published in the journal *Learning & Behaviour* in 2018: "We found that dogs not only sense what their owners are feeling; if a dog knows a way to help them, they will go through barriers to provide help."

We know that "catching" a yawn – a sign of social empathy – is most frequent between dogs and humans, more than any other species, even those to whom we appear to be closely related. The question is whether this empathy between dogs and us has evolved over time, due to the mutual benefits such empathy has provided, or whether there is something of a divine plan at work here. Of course, the two aren't mutually exclusive.

Then, there is the further question of whether a dog *needs* to act according to its empathy, or whether it *chooses* to. At this point, are we not considering *love* as a possible incentive?

It won't surprise you to know that I believe our dogs are capable of love – feeling it and demonstrating it. Indeed, it could be argued that they demonstrate love in a purer way – a more selfless way – than most humans. If "greater love has no man than to lay down his life for his friends" (John 15:13), I have no doubt that Sophie would have done so for me, had the need risen – love as demonstrated by *Greyfriar's Bobby* or *Foxie* beneath Striding Edge, as they lay with their dead masters long after their natural instincts would have dictated.

And if we are contemplating the possibility that our dogs love, are we not closer to considering their presence with us in heaven?

I met two Sophie lookalikes on the Fells today and both made as much fuss of me as I did of them.

It was wonderful and highly therapeutic.

Love,

Nev.

4

A Load of Bull

Hi Nev,

I think you're right about our dogs *loving* us, especially if the word 'love' denotes selfless devotion. I'm sure in one of our chats, I have told you the story of my first black Lab, Mij. I had been ordained only a few days and started as a curate in a tough parish in Nottingham. I went out one afternoon for a jog with Mij along a public footpath next to a river that ran near my house. To my horror, a bull appeared out of some hedges and charged at me, its horns heading straight for my stomach. It hit me with such force that I was tossed into the air at least three feet. Its horns, mercifully, went either side of my waist (I was much leaner in those days!). The next thing I knew I was in the river, trying desperately to get my footing on the very muddy and slippery bottom below. The bull was coming down the bank, snorting, heading right for me.

At that moment, I saw Mij run up behind the bull and emit this primal howl – a noise I never heard from a Labrador before or since. She then leaped onto the bull's back and bit into his flanks. This caught his attention. He turned to try and attack Mij but Mij had already anticipated the manoeuvre and was sprinting down the path from which I had just been launched. The bull chased her, but Mij outran him. Meanwhile, I got some purchase at last on the bottom of the river and pushed myself to the opposite bank where I sat soaked and shocked. I had literally just got ordained and I almost hadn't made it to my first Sunday! That would probably have been a first in the annals of the Church of England!

Mij swam across the river and sat next to me on the wet grass, barking at the angry bull that had returned and was now opposite us, rutting at the riverbank. All this was witnessed by several locals and reported to the press. The next Sunday morning I awoke to headlines in most of the newspapers, my favourite of which was "Holy Cow!" I still have the black-and-white photo of Mij and me taken by the Daily Telegraph photographer. It shows me with hair!

If what Mij did for me isn't love, I don't know what is! If love is, at its purest, self-forgetful, then it surely qualifies. Some may argue that Mij was self-serving, not self-forgetful. Some evolved survival instinct kicked in and my dog knew that if her master perished, she might too. But that more Darwinian approach, while possible, fails to honour the mystery of what you and I know as *love*.

And here's the thing: I don't remember paying for a single drink in any of the pubs in my parish for the next four years. Within five days of starting my ministry as curate, nearly every one of the 17000 souls seemed to know who I was. Every time I went into a pub, I was greeted with, "Hello, Father. What'll it be?" Followed by people asking after my dog.

I can safely say it would have taken me decades of hard graft to have achieved that level of good will!

My God knew what he was about, and so did my dog!

I'm so pleased you met those two Sophie lookalikes!

What joy!

Love,

Mark.

Hi Mark,

I completed my project of climbing every 'Wainwright' Lake District fell this week. I finished on Walla Crag overlooking Derwent Water. I had saved it for last as it was an easy enough fell for Lesley to accompany me. The completion of a project that has taken over fourteen years was emotional, but as I took in the panoramic view of the mountains all around me, I realised that I had stood on the top of each one together with Sophie. As I explained that to Lesley, a sudden surge of grief burst out and I sobbed – again! It caught me quite by surprise, as I thought I had begun to come to terms with her not being with me. I'm not sure what the other people on the top made of it all! It just reminds me that the happiest of days have been shared with her.

I come back to that sense of loss, and the thoughts of our dogs being part of who we are (or at least how we see ourselves). I feel incomplete without Sophie around. Perhaps that is a sign that more redemptive healing is required, yet I think the gift of companionship that our dogs represent says something about the fact that God has made us to be more than just our individual selves. And here's the thing: I still have the same conversations that I had with her, but now with the One who is alongside me, but unseen.

Please don't misunderstand me here, I didn't ever confuse Sophie with the Holy Spirit, but it appears that the Holy Spirit is just as interested in the sort of stuff about which I would witter on to Sophie, as well as all the 'important' stuff.

Perhaps, in Sophie, He has been listening all along.

Nev.

5

Luther's Pup

Hi Nev,

I'm glad you got to sob again. Does grief ever stop catching us by surprise? I have moments to this day when memories of canine loss are triggered by the most unexpected things. As you say, our dogs become a part of us, leaving us feeling incomplete when they are gone. And as for talking with our dogs, yes, I plead guilty. I talk with Bella too, especially on walks. In fact, she looks forlorn when I don't. When I speak to her when we're out, her tail wags and she seems uplifted, especially now she is getting older.

I do think there's a very interesting connection between talking to our dog and talking with God (prayer). This, for me, works at so many levels. When I was a vicar, my Black Lab Molly went everywhere with me. In staff meetings on Tuesday mornings, she would lie at my feet. When I led the team in prayer, she would wag her tail every time I said the name Jesus. One time, I remember someone lying on the floor in great pain, receiving prayer for healing with the laying on of hands. Molly rested her two front paws gently on the person's arm.

So, yes, while I agree that interacting with our dogs can teach us how to pray, I also think that the way our dogs interact with us can teach us more about prayer too. This must be one of the reasons why God has placed canine companionship as a gift within His creation. Just as Jesus is my Master, so I am my dog's Master. Bella seems to live to please me (Cherith says she is *obsessed* with me!). She follows me everywhere, even into the toilet (Bella, not Cherith!). She wags when she hears my voice. She shakes with joy when I play with her.

I think we could learn a lot about prayer from our interaction with our dogs, not only from the way we speak to them, but also from their eagerness for our presence and their attentiveness to our voice. In *Table Talk,* we read this: "When Martin Luther's puppy happened to be at the table, it looked for a morsel from his master, and watched with open mouth and motionless eyes. Luther said, 'Oh, if I could only pray the way this dog watches the meat! All his thoughts are concentrated on the piece of meat. Otherwise, he has no thought, wish, or hope'."

God, make us more like Luther's puppy!

With you in the tears, my friend,

Love,

Mark.

Dear Mark,

I think I remember Molly. I remember being rather excited to see the presence of a dog in the 'green room' at St. Andrews, when you were the vicar there. I was disappointed that, in the main, no-one was really bothered. I thought, "But there's a dog in here! Why isn't everyone giving her the intention she deserves, and fussing over her?" People were going about their business as if she wasn't there, and they're supposed to be godly people! I admit to being a little more focussed on the dog than the prayers that day. I think Jesus understood, though.

I talk a little about our relationship as 'master' to our dogs in my book *Dying to Meet You – The Gospel of Surrender & Grace*. Sophie's life was so much better for the fact that she delighted in me being her master. It is one of the reasons why her ashes are still with me here in my office, as opposed to having been scattered on one of the fells. At the end of the day, her favourite place of all was as close to me as possible. I think we are the few of the few who love our dogs so much that we even let them into the toilet with us. She knew me so well that she knew when it was time for me to go!

What I am still having to learn, is that Jesus's favourite place of all is as close to me as possible. My life message is "the one thing necessary" that Mary had found (Luke 10:42), so I understand that our favourite place should be at Jesus's feet. Yet, to understand that Jesus loves to be that close to me is still something that I need to make more central to my being.

In my meditations, I have often asked the question, "What will He say to me as I enter heaven?" The reply? "It's SO good to see you." I picture *His* delight that I am there with Him – the Father throwing His arms around me. Is that one of the reasons we love our dogs so much, that they delight in us more than we delight in ourselves?

Nev.

6

My Master

My dear Nev,

I was interested in what you said about the 'green room' at St Andrew's (although, when I was the vicar there we never gave it that name!). It always fascinated me who did and didn't interact with Molly. I know I need to allow for the fact that some people are afraid of dogs, often because of trauma, but what always most concerned me was not fear but indifference. Dogs are a kind of gateway creature; they reveal the extent to which we're connected with – or *desire* to connect with – the larger natural world beyond our often-disconnected urban lives. That much, I think, is a given. What is less recognized is the fact that these same adorable creatures are also gateways to something more spiritual, to the supernatural world of God's love.

As you know, John Wesley led the greatest revival Great Britain has ever witnessed – a revival that began with his heart being "strangely warmed". Thereafter, he saw an astonishing spiritual awakening everywhere he rode his horse. One of the things that he looked for in the newly awakened was their attitude towards dogs. Dogs were either ignored or mistreated. They fended for themselves, roaming the streets, searching for scraps. When Wesley saw revival breaking out, he said that he could always tell when someone had received a genuinely life-transforming experience of God's love by the way they now treated dogs. Their compassion for animals, especially dogs, for Wesley was one of the distinguishing hallmarks of the Spirit!

I think there's so much in what you say about Sophie delighting in just being with you. A dog's delight in being with their master is a crucial piece of testimony when we consider the question you and I are moving towards – do dogs go to heaven? Answering this will bring me to my favourite sermon by John Wesley. But that will have to wait another day. In the meantime, I understand why you keep Sophie's ashes close to you. The bond, in a very real sense, can never be broken.

May the everlasting arms continue to hold you in comfort.

With love,

Mark.

Dear Mark,

Welcome home! I trust you had a good time in Northern Ireland.

Quite frankly, I will admit that I am quick to judge those who are indifferent to animals in general, and dogs especially. I just know, from the outset, we are not going to get on. That judgement extends to those who are indifferent to the beauty of the world around them. My days in the countryside and on the fells are, first and foremost, days of worship; I cannot help but be inspired by God's creative genius to praise Him. In that inspiration, a heart to care and to cherish is born. To my mind, indifference to God's creation and His creatures reveals an indifference to the character – the 'nature' – of the One in whom, by whom, and for whom all things were created.

I was reminded, this week, of how mankind was given dominion over the earth and all living creatures. After the flood, that dominion was reinstated, but through fear. The very special relationship that we have with our dogs speaks of a greater restoration of the relationship between man and creation, where fear is removed, and creation rejoices in our dominion, as we have been restored – recreated – to be the 'masters' we were supposed to be, in the image of our Father. It is such a joy to have a dog who delights in being 'mastered' by me. In fact, for Sophie, it defined her existence; I completed her. That relationship, I believe, is a promise of how it will be when "all things are made new" – when we worship together with all creation in unity and harmony. And now I'm in danger of sounding a bit like a hippy!

If our dogs are part of the promise – the first fruits – how could it be that they will *not* be in the new heaven and earth that is to come?

And, with that, I'm heading out to the fells again . . .

Nev.

7

In The Garden

Ah, I love this Nev. The fact that we are returning to the beginning before we deal with the end. That appeals to the storyteller in me. When I write a novel, I always return to the questions/problems raised at the start of the story when I attend to the final Act. I need to make sure that the questions I raised in Act 1 are addressed again in Act 3, hopefully with a true and satisfying sense of resolution.

That's why I want to spend a bit more time on the beginning, on the Garden, where God and humans were friends, and where humans and animals were too. I must confess my nervousness though about *dominion*. There is so much colonial thinking around this idea in Christian circles, especially ones dominated by white patriarchy. There, dominion sounds like domination.

I must say that I am profoundly allergic to this thinking. It leads far too easily to master-slave language when men in this kind of constituency preach about God's mandate to have dominion over creation and to occupy every sphere of society. That sounds like *gentrification* to me. Too easily it has led historically to oppressing other races as slaves and treating animals as mere commodities. No thank you.

However, in a single *master*stroke, you have rescued and redeemed the word 'master' from the oppressors. In your last email, you spoke about Sophie rejoicing in your role as her master because your default setting in relation to her was always one of love, tenderness, kindness, equality, servanthood, and above all friendship – deep, spiritual, unitive, marvellous friendship.

This surely was the Father's intention in the beginning of the human story, that we should be masters and mistresses to the animal world, and to the natural world in general, seeing the birds and the trees as our brothers and sisters, as Saint Francis did, not seeking to dominate and colonise them but to serve and love them, bringing them into true adoration of the Creator.

I love this way of thinking. And you are right: every time someone like you invests time in loving a dog like Sophie, and every time you invite the fells into your gratitude to the divine artist who painted such extreme beauty, this is not just a re-enactment of the bond we had at the beginning, but a foretaste of the unbridled joy and connection we will have again at the end.

Thank you so much for that thought, that we are servant masters, loving masters, liberating masters, not lords of domination. We are fired by the power of love, not the love of power. That is a redemptive thought. You have reclaimed 'master' from the enslavers and have placed it again in the hands and on the lips of the emancipators. A true glimpse of heaven!

Sophie was very blessed.

With love,

Mark.

Dear Mark,

> *'For a child has been born to us, a son is given to us; he will*
> *bear the **symbol of dominion** on his shoulder, and his title*
> *will be: Wonderful Counsellor, Mighty Hero, Eternal Father,*
> *Prince of Peace. Wide will be the dominion and boundless*
> *the peace bestowed on David's throne and on his kingdom,*
> *to establish and support it with justice and righteousness*
> *from now on, for evermore.'* (Isaiah 9: 6-7)

The Old Testament prophet Isaiah foresaw the redemption of the principle of dominion as, I believe, he saw what it was that Jesus bore on His shoulders – the cross. The lordship (*dominus*) that's fashioned in God's image, and that Adam forfeited, is regained by Jesus on the cross – the ultimate act of trust in the Father, and sacrifice of self.

I am in total agreement with you when you say that *dominion* sounds like domination, for that is how men have chosen to 'lord' it over each other, as well as the earth and its creatures. Yet, Jesus shows us how to be *dominus* – the humble, servant-hearted, and loving lord befitting a true son and heir to the Father's domain, His Kingdom.

I bring all this into how we have been examining the way in which our relationship with our dogs reflects the nature of our relationship with the Father. My desire was always to give Sophie the best life she could possibly have every day. Sophie understood and trusted me in that – even with procedures that might have seemed to be hurtful and harmful. Her trust in my love and my ability to care for her meant that she was willing to submit to what I was doing with her – or to her – even though it was beyond her understanding. I think that is what upsets me about having her put to sleep; she was faithfully and submissively trusting me, even to the point of death. Though I know it was for her best, I can't help but feel that was something of a betrayal.

My desire, of course, was never to 'lord' it over her, and that is why our relationship was so special; our dogs respond to Father-like lordship. One only needs to look at the 'master' to see why so many dogs are dangerous or display anti-social behaviour: any obedience is gained only through fear. Dogs seem to understand and respond to genuine love and care. They thrive on it and are then content to live within the boundaries (or domain) that we set for them. In fact, they *need* to live within them.

So, to the Garden. I believe that while man was content to live under God's dominion, he was able to be the *dominus* that creation desired and needed. Yet our desire for independence caused creation to be independent of us. Dogs appear to be a 'sign' of how to put that right! If we could only trust and submit to our loving Master (who much prefers to be known as Father), in the same way that our dogs are towards us, will we not taste something of Eden restored?

What joy that will be!

Nev.

8

True Friends

Dear Nev,

I hear you. I have come across remote (aloof) as well as relational dog owners. What I'm calling the remote ones sometimes even put their dog on a chain. I have seen this from Northern Ireland to Uganda. They leave their dogs outside shackled to a post. In their eyes, the dog is a kind of servant. Its presence is purely dependent on its usefulness. The poor creature is generally neglected and afraid. However, the relational dog owner takes a very different view. They look after and love their animal, not through the lens of some utilitarian goal but simply because the animal to them is not a slave but a friend and will forever be cherished and remembered as that.

Here's where I get to the part of your email that it's taken me days and nights to muster up the courage to consider. When it comes to that dreadful choice – the choice whether to allow our beloved dog to continue in suffering or to fall asleep in our arms – the remote owner does not hesitate. The creature has outlived its purpose. It is time for it to go. The relational person, on the other hand, is devastated. The choice is traumatic. As you said, we know that this is for the best, but as they lie in our arms looking up at us with those trusting eyes we cannot help feeling that somehow we are robbing them of something by making this terrible choice on their behalf.

I have been reflecting why we feel this way. Maybe it's because most relational dog owners would happily give their life for their friend. Greater love hath no man than this, after all, that he lay down his life for his friend. And why not the friend that walks at our heels, following our shadow wherever it moves? We cannot abide the idea that we are powerless in this most gut-wrenching moment, that we cannot somehow find a new treatment, or even take their place. We know they would do it in a heartbeat for us, like when Mij attacked the bull that was trying to kill me. But now, when it's our turn, we can do nothing except watch those precious eyes lose their sparkle.

In the end, there will always be people who misinterpret the divine mandate to have 'dominion' as an invitation to control and to enslave. They are the most wretched of people. But then there are those who see it as it really is, an invitation from the God of love to say to the animal world what Jesus said to his own disciples, "I no longer regard you as servants but as friends." There will always be people for whom dominion means treating humans and animals in a way that evokes fear. But the hope for the world lies in those who have learned from their dog and their God that true redemption lies in treating each other as friends to love, come what may.

My love to you, especially as you think about Sophie and her last moments.

I'm sure when we all meet again she will thank you.

Mark.

Dear Mark,

Well, that set me off again! Your final comment reminds me of something I have experienced this week. As much as we might have hope, or even belief, there is, of course, so much more power in *hearing* the truth first hand. In one of my morning devotions this week, I read a line (an antiphon from the daily Psalter of Divine Office) that I heard in my spirit as if the Father had spoken directly to me. It was a simple, basic truth – one that is fundamental to our Christian faith – but it was made more real because it came direct from the Source. Likewise, your comment that Sophie will thank me carried with it such authority that I could almost hear her say it.

Communication with creation is one of my longings – to convey to it that I am, indeed, its friend. I remember watching *Jackanory* as a child and being particularly taken with a story about a boy who discovered that he could communicate with his dog telepathically. I spent the next few weeks desperately trying to do the same with our Golden Labrador. At times, I was convinced there was a connection between us that no-one else understood! However, even now, I talk to any animal I pass on my walks and am thrilled when there is a response that shows that there may be some understanding, on their part, that there is no need to be afraid – hence my delight when the cows next door to us began to trust me enough to lick my hand, the pleasure I feel helping a lamb in distress, and for it not to then run off but stay with me, allowing me to stroke it, or even the comfort of knowing that a pair of coal tits feel safe enough to nest in our garden wall.

I suspect that all animal lovers like us would love to be a Dr Doolittle. What we most want to say is that there is no need to fear us – "we are one of you." We want to be accepted by them and for them to understand that we love and care for them.

Thinking back to the Garden, that 'friendship' was inherent in the order of creation. I wonder if there was even an ability to communicate one with another. After all, Adam and Eve don't seem to have been phased by a talking snake (Ricky Gervais take note!).

Once again, it is our dogs who give us a glimpse into that friendship with all creation – a taste of what was lost and a foretaste of that which will be restored. I truly believe that I will hear Sophie speak her thanks to me one day. Perhaps she will remind me of all the other conversations between us that I didn't realise she had understood so clearly.

Love to the three of you,

Nev.

9

Heal/Heel!

Dear Nev,

I am very struck by these thoughts about our oneness with the natural world, and indeed our responsibility not to control and coerce using fear, but to serve and bless using love. You may not know this about me, but I have something of a history when it comes to praying for animals. I have always been one to lay my hand on an animal's head and bless it. When I was vicar of St Andrew's Chorleywood, there was always at least one Labrador guide dog in the congregation. I would always give her or him communion when I came to the dog's master, asking first of course. No one ever turned the offer down and the dog concerned would always take the bread with great dignity. I stopped short of administering the wine, obviously, but I am amazed that I was never excommunicated and defrocked. If I had been threatened with it, I would have simply pleaded that we are called to be priests for animals as much as priests for people. If they had argued, I would simply have pointed them towards the many stories surrounding St Francis and his brothers and sisters in the animal world.

And it didn't stop there either. I have sometimes felt compelled by God's love to pray for the healing of sick animals. One of my most vivid memories was when I was the vicar of a parish on the edge of Sheffield. There was a man there who I really wanted to know our Heavenly Father's love. He was not a churchgoer but was very open to me as a person. I visited him one afternoon while doing my rounds and saw his Black Labrador – whom he adored – lying on the floor just beyond the threshold to his house. The dog looked lethargic. My friend looked teary. "I've just heard," he said. "Cancer. Inoperable. Just a matter of days." To see this big bloke in such a state broke my heart, as did the dog's obvious distress. "May I pray for her?" I asked. He nodded. I knelt. Placed my hand on her head. Prayed a simple prayer for healing. Blessed the dog and her owner and left. A while later, the man told me he'd been to the vet. The dog was completely healed. I have never forgotten the joy in his face, nor the joy in my heart.

Furthermore – and here I may stretch your faith to the very limit – this gift even extends to cats! Yes, cats! Our closest friends here in Kent have a rescue cat. Over many years, they have succeeded in restoring the animal's trust in human beings. The transformation, which Cherith and I have witnessed, is quite remarkable. The cat was so frightened of everyone, including them. Now, he's the opposite – trusting, talkative, affectionate, quirky, delightful.

A few years ago, they were told he was very severely ill and would not survive. When they went away for a brief holiday, I offered to go over and sit with him. I took chicken that I had roasted just for him – to help him trust me enough to do what he had never allowed before, lay my hand on his little head. I prayed for his healing, and he purred (Amen?). He made an instant recovery and is still, against all odds, with us, happier and healthier than ever! As I said to our friends, "I'm useless when it comes to praying for humans to be healed. But animals . . . that seems to work much better." Maybe I love animals more than I do humans.

I think there's something in all this, and in the beautiful thoughts you shared about cows and lambs.

It's all very redemptive.

Love,

Mark.

Dear Mark,

Oh, I love this! Animal healing stories! Although I wonder if it was more a case of deliverance with the cat!

My childhood career option was to be a vet but sadly I was not disposed to the sciences. That said, I'm not sure it would be possible to love animals in the way that I do and be a vet. Perhaps it would just be too traumatic.

Your stories remind me of my own story of dog healing. Chester lived until he was 17. In his later years, he went completely deaf, possibly reaping the results of the countless occasions when he had feigned deafness in his more independent years. The vet confirmed it – clapping his hands above and around Chester's head with no response. At that time, our kids were much younger, and played in the cul de sac where we lived with many other children who all got to know Chester. They knew that if they wanted his attention, they would have to come up to him and catch his eye rather than just call him.

During one of my morning devotions, I quite unexpectedly felt the prompting of the Holy Spirit to lay my hands over Chester's ears and speak healing to them. This I did with no obvious effect. A while later, we suddenly noticed that Chester started to react to the doorbell, as he had done when he was younger. He was able to hear us when we called him, to the delight of all the children who played outside. I still remember their excitement, running around shouting, "Chester can hear" and calling his name repeatedly – something with which, in true Chester fashion, he soon got very bored and sought sanctuary with me.

Of course, this posed a question. I took it back into my prayer time: "Why heal my dog when I pray for him, but not the people in the church when I pray for them?" Immediately, the answer came back: "Because you love your dog." Over the years I have pondered that answer. I believe the healing came because I responded to the Holy Spirit's promptings in the moment. It was not because the strength of my love (or indeed faith) had anything to do with getting my prayers answered.

The question (and answer) still stands as to why the Father chose to heal Chester's ears. He knows the desires of our hearts. He chooses the very best gifts for us, always out of love and sometimes with no other motive than to bless.

Another argument for the presence of our dogs in heaven, I think.

Nev.

10

Perfection

Dear Nev,

Apologies for the late reply. I have had the funeral for my oldest friend and have been much preoccupied with that, and with memories of him. The thanksgiving service yesterday was inspiring and uplifting. My friend was lauded by his former employers for his combination of comedy and compassion. What a duet! And I can confirm that he had both in abundance. He was always the embodiment of that old definition of true friendship: the true friend is someone who walks in when the rest of the world walks out. I have no doubt that he is in heaven, and that the great beyond is louder with the sound of his laughter. And, of course, the sound of barking and sighing from all the dogs we have loved and lost, such as your beloved Chester and Sophie.

It's a fascinating question this, isn't it — do dogs go to heaven? A vicar friend of mine, Tom, suffered the loss of his beautiful black Labrador Archie nine months ago. He wrote a private message to me on Instagram.

"Hey, Mark! What's your theology of our Black Labs being part of the new creation or heaven?"

I know it may sound a little abstract, but I thought of the 11th century theologian Anselm of Canterbury and his classic argument for the existence of God. His rational argument for God's existence is very famous; God is "that than which nothing greater can be conceived." I remembered one part of his argument: God is the greatest possible being that can be imagined. I took that thought and applied it to heaven. I wrote this back to Tom.

"Well, it's a v good question. I believe that heaven must by definition be a state of being no greater than which can be conceived. I'm borrowing from Anselm in my language here (you'll recognise it from his argument for the existence of God). Heaven cannot be the greatest conceivable state of being if Black Labradors aren't at the gates to greet us and at our feet to soothe us. Therefore, Archie and Bella will be in heaven. Otherwise, heaven will be imperfect, and that's inconceivable."

Tom replied, "Thanks Mark! I'm working through this . . . I woke up at 6am as usual and sat downstairs and was broken by the deafening silence. No deep sigh or clank of his nametag hitting the laminate floor. His presence gone. I have loved that dog for 12 years and he was such a companion. The grief is so real . . . what a blessing Labradors really are . . ."

I don't know if my words comforted Tom. All I know is this: I cannot imagine heaven being perfect if our dogs are not there because their absence would introduce a critical flaw into what is perfect. Also, and this is another argument altogether, the dogs that I have loved are in so many ways better (i.e., more loving creatures) than most of the humans I have known. They are more *unconditionally* loving. They are more faithful. They are more perfect pictures of devotion.

The words we use of our greatest human friends we could also use of our dogs (they are comedians and comforters in equal measure, aren't they?). I think that this is the reason why the great Robert Louis Stevenson had it right: "You think dogs will not be in heaven? I tell you they will be there long before any of us!"

I find it hard to disagree with him.

I'm sure you feel the same.

Love,

Mark.

Dear Mark,

My heart goes out to you; losing a friend has its own unique grief. I guess we are approaching that stage in life when losing our friends becomes something with which we will become more acquainted but, so far, I have only experienced the loss of one of my 'peers'. In fact, the last time I was in St. Andrews Chorleywood was to give a eulogy for my friend Les Hall – truly a friend with whom I laughed a great deal. I'm sure you would agree that laughter makes a friendship, and certainly maintains it. I can't think of a friend with whom I can't have a laugh; the two go hand in hand. I am challenged by that fact in thinking about my friendship with Jesus. Sometimes, it feels as if there should be more play and less effort, more fun and less seriousness. I love a good deep contemplation, but I wonder if I am missing out on something of the fun of the friendship at times.

It certainly is a fascinating subject that we are considering. What begins with a seemingly innocent and (some would say) childish question leads us into the deepest of thoughts concerning our hope. It causes us to reflect on the character of our Father and how He is reflected in His own creation. I think that your argument as presented in your last email has always been what has convinced me of the presence of our dogs in heaven. Heaven just could not be heaven without them. However, the more I think on this, that argument is expanded by asking, "Well, why would He leave them out?" Surely, what He created was "very good," not "B minus, could do better." It was us who spoilt it. Yes, He will be our All in all throughout eternity and we won't *need* our dogs to make up for a lack in our ability to love and be loved (of which some might accuse us). I believe our dogs will be there just because they have always been such a good idea! My hope is that our friendship with them will be more than we have been able to have here.

Following the loss of Chester, I had a dream a couple of weeks later – a dream that has remained with me as if it were a memory.

I arrived at a kind of reception room for heaven – literally a reception room as beyond this room there was a celebration going on. For me, as an introvert, arriving for any event where I don't know quite what to expect is always stressful, which is why I generally head for the kitchen with my bottles, and wedge myself in between worktops with, at least, some control over who talks to me!

However, on arriving at this reception, I was greeted by someone I recognised, but couldn't quite place – a person, yet not a person like us; different in some way but still able to converse and interact as we do. He looked at me and smiled, clearly seeing that I was confused as to who he was.

He said, "It's me. Chester!"

With that, he led me into the party.

At which point I woke up.

I still remember that feeling of joy as I recognised him. Once he identified himself, I could see that it was obvious that it was him. I just hadn't expected him to be more like us!

On waking, I was utterly convinced, and I still am, that I had met him as he is (or will be).

I look forward to being met by him again but being ready for it next time.

There is so much, between him and Sophie, that we will have to talk about.

Now that might just be a party I could enjoy!

What a fantastic hope.

Or a realistic one?

Nev.

11

Chester's Dream

Morning Nev,

Thanks for your kind words. Just as an aside, during the meal after my late friend's thanksgiving, an elderly and eccentric chap from my first curacy in Nottingham came and said hello. His name is Robert. He smiled and said, "We all remember you from your time as curate at St Helen's." I thought he was going to add something about my preaching, or my visiting skills with the housebound, but he didn't mention them, or anything else that might have cast a good light on me. Instead, he grinned – revealing many more gaps than I remember – and said cheerily, "You're famous. You were attacked by that bull. It got into the papers. Never forgotten it." I smiled limply back, my ego even more crushed than it already was! "Oh, thank you . . . I think," I said, unsure whether this was a good thing to be known for or not!

I was moved reading about your dream of Chester as a talking, almost human creature. I am sure that many surprises await us in the new earth, the new creation. I think the artists and in particular the storytellers, being of a more mystical temperament than most, have occasionally glimpsed something of these future mysteries. You know that my dad was a star pupil and friend of C.S. Lewis and dined with him most Tuesday nights while Dad was an undergraduate at Merton College, Oxford (where Tolkien was based too). Lewis of course has talking animals in Narnia, which in its redeemed state (governed by the four children who have passed through the wardrobe door) is a heavenly vision. There are nearly twenty breeds of dogs mentioned in the Narnia Chronicles, including Border Collies (yes, Sophie!).

I am probably moving too far forward here, in relation to our topic that is, because I'm assuming that talking animals will be a part of the new creation/new earth after the return of Jesus, just as they are in Narnia. We will need to spend more time on whether they are or not. But let's assume they are and let's consider whether they will be different from what we see on the earth today. I propose that the answer is yes. We know that Jesus, after he had experienced resurrection from the dead on the first Easter morning, was both similar and dissimilar to what he had been before. The disciples had trouble recognizing him after his resurrection. Once they realized who he was, they knew without any doubt that he was the Risen Lord – even Thomas did. So, there was both continuity and discontinuity.

We also know that the same will be true of us. When we are raised from the dead at the sound of the last trumpet, we will be both like and unlike who we are now. We will have glorious, spiritual, incorruptible, resurrection bodies and this will mean that we both look like, and don't look like, what we are today. Most importantly of all, we will look like our former selves, yes, but we will also look more like Jesus than we have before. The Apostle John knew this full well which is why he stresses in one of his letters in the New Testament (1 John 3:2): "Dear friends, now we are children of God, and what we will be has not yet been made known. But we know that when Christ appears, we shall be like him, for we shall see him as he is."

So, I return to your beloved Chester. In your dream, he was both like the Chester you had known and loved, and unlike him. But once you had recognized him, you knew it was him! I wonder if this will be true of everything in the new creation/new earth. Everything – the trees, the mountains, the cattle, the fields, the sky, the stars, the sea, the fish, and especially our dogs – will be both like and unlike, both continuous and discontinuous, with their former form. Maybe this is why the Apostle John describes "one *like* an ox," "one *like* a lion," one *like* a man", "one *like* a flying eagle", surrounding God's throne in heaven and praising the Creator. Notice the word "like". John doesn't say this is what they are. He says this is what they're *like*. In the new earth, everything has undergone a divine metamorphosis.

I think while we are here, living on the old earth, we must resort to similes when we think of heaven. There will be animal-**like** creatures in heaven. The Apostle John tells us so. And he goes on to tell us (this is all in the latter part of Revelation chapter 4), that they speak! They declare that God is Holy. They say it three times – Holy, Holy, Holy. Obviously, this is because they are praising the three persons of the Godhead, each one deemed holy – as indescribably and perfectly pure.

Maybe this is where dream-Chester was leading you. Maybe what lay beyond the reception room was this celebration, this party of all parties, that John is straining to portray in Revelation 4. I love the thought of all our dogs being involved, joining with us in a joy that is both spoken and unspeakable!

Maybe even the bull that once attacked me will be there – restored and redeemed!

After all, as your man in Revelation 4 says, around the throne there's one like an ox!

Love,

Mark.

Dear Mark,

This is fascinating. Since having that dream of Chester, I have been able to understand why the Apostle John describes the creatures that he sees in heaven in the way that he does in the Book of Revelation. It's just too difficult to adequately describe what we 'see' in the heavenly realm. Our spiritual eyes accept realities that our physical minds can't process. So, to use my Chester dream as an example, he was 'like' a man but not a man, and yet I cannot describe how he was unlike a man, except that I understood that he was not! Now it is all beginning to sound like something Lewis Carroll might write. That which is nonsense here, may well make good sense in heaven.

I have never researched how it was that C.S. Lewis came to 'discover' Narnia. Was it all his own (divinely inspired) brilliant creation to illustrate his understanding of the heavenly realm? Or had he had some kind of experience from which to draw? I would love to ask him how much of Narnia he considered fantasy as opposed to heavenly reality or possibility.

In Genesis chapter 2, we see God forming the wild animals and birds, bringing them to 'the man' in response to His declaration, "It is not good for the man to be alone; I shall make a partner suited to him." God brings all the animals to the man for him to *name* them. Does this not speak of an intended relationship and communication between man and the animals that was present before the fall? Is it too much of a stretch to glean this from the poetic mythology of Genesis? If communication and relationship were part of the natural order in Eden, I believe it would be likely that this would be replicated – if not enhanced – in the new Eden. We know that there will be a unity in heaven beyond our earthly comprehension – all things united in Christ, all things united in worship and adoration. Is it possible to have unity without communication?

I may be leaping too far ahead here as, rather than merely considering the possibility of the presence of our dogs in heaven, I am already convinced we will be able to talk with them there, as well as worship together!

Perhaps, at some stage, we need to look at the arguments that might be made for our dogs *not* being in heaven, so that we can make every effort to discount them.

Back to you then!

Nev.

12

After Life

Dear Nev,

You're right. We do need to address the arguments against dogs being in heaven. I suspect religious people who make them may be guilty in part of double standards – believing that heaven exists, but that dogs cannot be a part of it. This seems to me to lack consistency. It proposes that there is an afterlife for humans, but not for the rest of creation. I think this derives from a false dualism between human beings (spiritual) and the rest of creation (material). The Hebrew Scriptures declare that the whole earth is the Lord's and everything in it. Everything in nature is touched, enriched, sustained by the Father's blessing, however marred and imperfect, just as every human being still bears the image of God, however depraved. I have always been a lover of Gerard Manly Hopkins's poetry. He wrote:

The world is charged with the grandeur of God.
  It will flame out, like shining from shook foil;
  It gathers to a greatness, like the ooze of oil
Crushed. Why do men then now not reck his rod?
Generations have trod, have trod, have trod;
  And all is seared with trade; bleared, smeared with toil;
  And wears man's smudge and shares man's smell: the soil
Is bare now, nor can foot feel, being shod.

And for all this, nature is never spent;
    There lives the dearest freshness deep down things;
And though the last lights off the black West went
    Oh, morning, at the brown brink eastward, springs —
Because the Holy Ghost over the bent
    World broods with warm breast and with ah! bright wings.

To that I say Amen! The whole earth is the Lord's and everything in nature is charged by a divine grandeur despite our industrial ravages of the earth and our callous disregard for the animal world. And this grandeur includes dogs, which is why the person who says that dogs don't have souls, but there is a heaven, cannot have their cake and eat it. For me these either-or dualisms make no sense, which is why I love what you said about the non-sense of heaven, of the Lewis Carrollian flavour of God's imagination when it comes to eternity. Maybe we will spar with playful Jaberwockies in what Rabelais called the "great perhaps." Whatever happens, we will have Paradise Regained, and that — as you say — must involve a restoration of our original unity with the animal world in the new heaven-on-earth.

I therefore reject the argument: a) we get to enjoy the afterlife but (b) dogs don't. Such an argument is based on a reductionist view that our Great Father loves human beings but not the rest of creation. That seems absurd and too anthropocentric — dangerous too because it can lead to all sorts of ecological neglect and abuse. At least with deep thinkers like Ricky Gervais, their atheism is consistent. Ricky loves animals, especially dogs, but he does not consider heaven intellectually plausible (see his amazing TV series *After Life*). Dogs therefore do not have souls, and heaven does not exist. This is all we have. So, hold your animals close and care for them with tenderness and respect. As he said on Twitter recently (05/04/2019), "If the kindest souls were rewarded with the longest lives, dogs would outlive us all."

As for Lewis, he's a great example of someone who embraced the spiritual and the material, the supernatural and the natural, in one holistic vision. Even the genesis of Narnia, which you asked about, reveals this integrity. The stories all began with him having what you and I would call prophetic dreams. It did not start with him saying, "I need to write a Christian allegory." It was far more mystical, intuitive than that. This is what he said (I have put in bold the words that suggest the operation of something prophetic):

> "All my seven Narnian books . . . began with seeing **pictures** in my head. At first they were not a story, just **pictures**. The Lion all began with a **picture** of a Faun carrying an umbrella and parcels in a snowy wood. This **picture** had been in my mind since I was about sixteen. Then one day, when I was about forty, I said to myself: "Let's try to make a story about it." At first I had very little idea how the story would go. But then suddenly Aslan came bounding into it. I think I had been having a good many **dreams** of lions about that time. Apart from that, I don't know where the lion came from or why He came. But once He was there he pulled the whole story together, and soon He pulled the six other Narnian stories in after Him. (*Of Other Worlds* p.42).

Narnia in part owes its origins to what you and I would call a spiritual or supernatural cause. But then there are material or natural influences too. One of the countless blessings of being married to a Northern Irish woman is that it's revealed how utterly ignorant we English are of all things Irish. I had no idea until I visited Rostrevor recently how much that stunning Northern Irish landscape – with its fine forests and sparkling lakes – had influenced Lewis's imagination. He grew up in Northern Ireland (until he was 10). In many ways, we think of him as an English writer, but the Irish have an even greater claim to make. And Narnia, however much it owes its existence to a supernatural cause, derives just as much from his love of this exquisite landscape, which he described as "my birthplace and dearest refuge."

I think I may have rambled away from the forest trail we were on at the end of your last email, so I'll try and find my way back. Chester and Sophie were not soulless creatures, destined only for the dust of the old earth. They were love-filled creatures, destined for the new heaven on earth at the end of the old earth's story and the start of the new.

You will see them again. You may not recognise them immediately. We will all have undergone a kind of metamorphosis that I believe is beyond the imaginations of the greatest poets, mystics, artists, and storytellers. But recognise them we will. And the landscape in which we play will be even finer than the lushest parts of Northern Ireland and Narnia combined.

Grace and peace.

Mark.

Good morning, Mark

Happy St. Eric's day!

I was in the land of the Prince Bishops yesterday, walking on the moors of the North Pennines, pondering our continuing discussion, and rejoicing in an even greater expectancy and excitement for the eternity that awaits us.

I was reminded of an occasion as a young teen in our evangelical (once Brethren) church, being concerned about whether our family dog, Shady (a Black Lab), would be going to heaven. As I was the only boy in the family, and because we lived a fair way away from both church and school, Shady was my best friend and playmate (I learned most of my rugby skills chasing her around the garden to get the ball from her, as she dodged and sprinted away just out of my diving grasp). What I was most reminded of was the condescending laughter with which my question was greeted. I expect, had anyone known that I was far more concerned about *her* being in heaven than any of *them*, the laughter may have changed to stern admonishment! I believe that much of the attitude of the scorners was down to sheer ignorance, born out of anthropocentric religious conditioning and the blinkered view that being a Christian was almost all and only about saving people from going to hell. It is a joy to be considering this subject now with you, and as I realised yesterday, there is even some healing in all of this from the religious shackles of the past.

The rather colourless Wayne Grudem in his *Systematic Theology* suggests that whether an animal has a soul simply depends on how we define *soul*. He states, "If we define 'soul' to mean 'the intellect, emotions and will' then we will have to conclude that at least the higher animals have a soul. But if we define our 'soul' to mean the immaterial element of our nature that relates to God and lives forever, then animals do not have a soul." Here we see again that anthropocentric inability to embrace the mystical union of Christ and His creation. How does he conclude that nature does not relate to God when, according to the poetic symbolism of Psalms and Isaiah, even inanimate creation such as trees and mountains "clap their hands" in praise-filled response to their Creator?

While we're on this topic, does the fact that animals have souls necessarily mean that those souls remain into eternity?

Are there certain animals with souls and others without?

If all have souls, will every animal that has ever lived be in heaven (or the new earth to be more accurate)?

I just don't know.

I turn again to our friend C.S. Lewis who supposed that pets "may have an immortality, not in themselves, but in the immortality of their masters." I have previously argued that our dogs have been *part* of us, in our friendship and mutual love. My knowledge of my Father's love suggests that, because of His love for me, His son, all that is pure and precious to me will be renewed with me into eternity. Our pets have taken on a special significance because of their place in our hearts – our souls. Perhaps, in the close bond with me that defined Sophie's earthly life, that had eternal consequences for her too.

I was delighted to read of the prophetic inspiration of Narnia for Lewis – especially the way Aslan burst onto the scene and united all things in him. If Lewis could have risen any higher in my estimation, he has done so! Perhaps, it was a faint taste of that inspiration that so moved me as I sat in his bedroom on our visit together.

My thanks to you.

I love this.

Nev.

13

Shady Lands

Dear Nev,

I love your story about Shady. Maybe her name was very significant! The problem with so much conservative religion is its unwillingness to find God's footprints (paw prints?) in the grey areas of life. Everything must fall into stark opposites, both morally and intellectually. The older I get, and the more I see of the suffering of God's creatures, the less inclined I am to talk about simple black-and-white solutions. It's not that they've broken down or fused (as in so much postmodernist philosophy), it's just that I find luminous signs of the Father's love in the shady, yes *shady*, areas of life – those places where answers are harder to come by, where there is ambiguity, where we walk with our dogs on a high mountain path between mystery and miracle.

I think this is why I find the conservative discussions about animal souls so prosaic – whether Catholic or Protestant. Grudem typifies a Protestant response, and you rightly use the word colourless. The classic Catholic response quotes Thomas Aquinas, beloved doctor of the Catholic church. He divided souls into vegetative, animal, and rational. Although it's undeniably subtle and stimulating, it's also ultimately dissatisfying because it doesn't seem to me to account for the finest attribute of the soul (soul understood as that part of a creature's being that has the capacity to reflect God's nature). That one great attribute is love. It is not the mind, intellect, and will that characterise the soul, nor is it the capacity to reason. It is the capacity to love.

This is what I think, no *believe*, confirms that Shady and Sophie will be in heaven. It is their capacity to love us that proves beyond any doubt in my mind that they have souls. That dogs love us is irrefutable. In fact, as Josh Billings once said, "a dog is the only thing on earth that loves you more than yourself." I agree. I would also state this: that dogs often love us with a greater love than we love each other. Dogs don't slag each other off on Twitter or leave scathing reviews on Amazon!

I think it was this realisation that brought James Thurber to the place where he could say that "if I have any beliefs about immortality, it is that certain dogs I have known will go to heaven, and very, very few persons." Although this is of course hyperbole, I do sympathise with the comment. My dogs have loved me better than most human beings!

Animals with the capacity to love us must therefore be said to have something of the divine within them. But we can go further than this. The Apostle John says that "God is love, and those who live in love live in God, and God lives in them!" If dogs — and other creatures — have the capacity to love, then God lives in them. God lives IN them. In THEM, not just in human beings. How arrogant we are to assume that only human beings can exhibit divine love! How *anthropocentric*, to use the word in your last message. Remember Saint Francis's donkey. When the beloved saint — who called animals his brothers and sisters — breathed his last breath, his donkey wept visible tears. Is that not love? How dare anyone say that this creature does not have a place in heaven?

And think about what kind of love the dog and the donkey call forth in us too! If these creatures can display such a divine virtue – the most beautiful of divine virtues – then why do we even pause to debate whether they go to heaven? Of course, they do. Is this not why Anatole France said that "until one has loved an animal, a part of one's soul remains unawakened?" That is one of the most profound statements ever made. Dogs awaken love in the human soul. We carry these stories of love with us throughout our lives. Memories of their unconditional love take up precious soul space, so that when we die, we bear them with us on the journey towards the Father's house – a house that is inconceivable without wagging tails.

In the end, it is not conservative piety that will provide answers to our main question, "Do dogs go to heaven?" The answers, if we can call them answers, will lie in a more mystical spirituality – one cultivated by those who are seized by a great affection for the natural world, and who see the natural world as the arena of the Father's blessing, not as a wilderness to be colonized or a resource to be plundered. And we shouldn't be at all worried about advocating for Christian mysticism. One of my favourite quotes over the last thirty years is from the great Jesuit theologian, Karl Rahner. He said this: "the Christian of the future will be a mystic, or they will not exist at all."

Last night we had a thunderstorm. Bella was shaking. I got out of bed, knelt over her, and covered her with my body. She stopped shaking while I held her. If I moved, she started to shake again.

It struck me that yet again our relationships with our dogs provide stunning pictures, enacted parables if you will, of the Great Father's love. In Jesus, God stepped down to our level, covered us, held us, and took our fears away. When I woke up this morning, Bella was sitting on the floor at my side of the bed, wagging and smiling — her way of saying thank you. That's our part, isn't it? Being grateful. Giving thanks. It's called worship.

Thank God for our dogs.

I write this in memory of Shady.

Love,

Mark.

Dear Mark,

I do so enjoy reading your emails — you write with such freedom and beauty — an amazing gift.

One of the many wonderful things that I have learned, as I have been mentored over the years by Guy Chevreau, is the necessity of being comfortable with and, indeed, embracing mystery. Most weeks we will have a deep couple of hours chewing the theological cud together in the understanding that there really are very few complete answers — only faith, hope and love. Guy and I so enjoy these conversations.

In our considerations of heaven, we are delving into mystery (possibly the greatest of them all) but there are clues that have been left for us and, as a former detective, I love following a trail of clues! It occurs to me that, if we want to know what heaven will be like, we should look at what we know of the Father. Will heaven not be a perfect expression of His character as all things will be filled with, and united in, His Son? Love, therefore, must be the most obvious and valuable aspect of heaven, for He *is* love. This was my suggestion way back in one of our first emails in this conversation. The very fact that our dogs so love us, and we so love them, must be sufficient qualification for their presence in heaven, as we only love because He loved us first (1 John 4:19). To love is to participate in the divine, and love is only possible because of that divine element in us. So, I agree, that the capacity to love must define the soul, as love is the greatest reflection and representation of who He is.

I loved how you comforted Bella in the storm. Such a beautiful picture; rather like a hen with her chicks (heard that before somewhere!). Once again you are presented with yet another 'dog parable' as an illustration of our relationship with the Father. In remembering my Chester dream, I realise that it was also a picture of how our dogs are used by God to lead us into a deeper understanding of who He is – *Chester led me* into the party.

Quite frankly, I haven't found a single argument of any substance against the presence of our dogs in heaven. It appears that, for the most part, the world of theologians has been rather indifferent on the subject. Back to that indifference that we find so suspicious in pious men and women.

Faith, hope, and love remain.

Nev.

14

In Memory of Tish

Dear Nev,

I love your comments about the indifference of pious folk. I had my own run in with one such. He was a queen's chaplain no less, taking the memorial service for a dear elderly friend of mine called Pauline. I loved Pauline, not least because of her affection for her dogs. She had border terriers all her life and, at least in my recollection, she called each one the same name – Tish! At her send off, the order of service had a photograph on the cover with Pauline and one of her many Tishes. I have many fond memories of Pauline puffing on her cigarette and Tish lying at her feet. Pauline and Tish rescued me at a particularly lonely time in my life, between school and university.

The queen's chaplain led and spoke at dear Pauline's memorial service. In his rather monotonous address, he mentioned that dogs have a universally bad image in the Bible. They were regarded as unclean and therefore not valued. I went up to him afterwards and said that this was only partially true. I reminded him of the parable of the rich man and the beggar called Lazarus. Lazarus sat outside the rich man's gates desperate for food, clothing, and basic medicinal help (he was covered in sores), while the rich man ate a daily feast with his brothers. Eventually, the beggar died and went to heaven. The rich man died and headed in the opposite direction.

I pointed out to the chaplain that Jesus mentions something very important about Lazarus before Lazarus dies. He says that "the dogs outside the rich man's gates licked Lazarus's sores." Most translations of the Bible say, *"even* the dogs licked his sores," suggesting that they were adding an additional woe to the beggar's torment. But this is a mistranslation. As my late friend Ken Bailey pointed out, the original Greek word does not mean "even". It means "but", as in "by way of contrast." The meaning is clear. Unlike the men inside the house, the dogs outside showed Lazarus compassion. While the men stuffed their mouths, the dogs licked the beggar's sores.

I once gave a talk at Wembley called "If we don't, the dogs will." I made the point that what we see here is Jesus taking a completely different view of dogs from his contemporaries. In his culture, dogs were not valued at all, but in his parable, dogs are the only ones that have compassion for the beggar. They don't see him as a "bum" who deserves to be out on his luck – which is the way some American Christians speak about the homeless. The dogs in the parable are street angels. They are performing healing on the streets. They are the only ones who minister comfort to the beggar.

I told this to the queen's chaplain; he didn't seem impressed!

I, on the other hand, remembering the Queen's love for her dogs, thought it was something he really should be exploring! I think she would have loved this reading of the parable.

And there's more!

Ken Bailey also reminds us that in the ancient world it was a well-known fact that the saliva of a healthy dog contained natural healing properties. Often dogs were used at healing spas in antiquity. That's why archaeologists discovered the bones of 1500 dogs at the sight of a healing centre associated with Asclepius, the Greek god of healing. Those who tended the sick knew that dogs were agents of alternative health care. Jesus knew it too. That's why he portrays the dogs licking Lazarus's wounds. They were not harming him (as our English translations wrongly imply); they were helping him.

Dogs are angels with healing in their tongues!

Love,

Mark.

Dear Mark,

Sorry for the delay. We have been away for the weekend celebrating the 25th anniversary of Betel UK. Wonderful to be amongst the hundreds of tattoos, scars, and absent teeth, in passionate worship and thankfulness for the many victories of rescued lives. That's real church.

As for your conversation with the chaplain, I react rather badly to those who appear aloof and dismissive. It is why I have an aversion to some golf clubs – full of exclusivity and self-importance. The love and care of a pet exhibits just the opposite of these most distasteful of traits.

I was deeply struck by what you have to say about Lazarus, and the dogs licking his sores. Knowing that Jesus was not in the business of making throwaway comments, even in the telling of a story, this must have truth for us to take on board. As you say, "If we don't, the dogs will." But is He saying more than that? Is He saying, "the dogs *do*" – that this is one of the reasons why He has put them here? Later in the parable (v.25), Abraham says of Lazarus, "Now he has his consolation here . . ." The consolation that the dogs provided Lazarus while on earth is now completed and perfected in heaven.

For many of us who have had such a close relationship with them, our dogs have provided the consolation that we have needed as life has dealt out its cruelty to us – consolation for loneliness or rejection, consolation for the love that we have not (but should have) received from those of our own species. Frankly, I am not sure I would have been able to have got through this life without that consolation. For the dogs to have been licking Lazarus, there must have been some mutual trust and affection. Not only would they have provided relief and healing for his sores, but for his heart also.

The dogs *were* his consolation and "now he has his consolation here . . ." Is it too much of a stretch to suggest that Jesus was leaving us a hint here? I think that this is exactly what Jesus was saying for people like you and me who have been so blessed to have known this consolation. This consolation, that has gone by the name of Molly or Shady, Mij or Chester, Bella or Sophie, we will have with us, completed and perfected in heaven.

I am sure of it.

Nev.

15

Consolation

Dear Nev

How wonderful to be at Betel's 25th! I remember Betel well from my time in Watford when I ran my former charity, the Father's House Trust. Betel has done extraordinary work among the most vulnerable in our society, especially on the streets. And that brings me back to the dogs that brought consolation to Lazarus, the homeless man in Jesus's story. I love the word you use – "consolation." That is precisely what those dogs provided for him. When the rest of the world walks out, dogs walk in. When we are beyond human compassion, we are never beyond the reach of canine consolation. Homeless people today will teach us this . . . if we have ears to hear.

In a recent edition of *The Big Issue*, Michelle Clark was interviewed. She is the woman who founded and runs DOTS, Dogs on the Streets. Have you heard of her/them? She helps to care for dogs when their homeless owners need to be taken into hospital or into accommodation that is not pet-friendly. She and her charity do a wonderful job. One of the men whose story she told is called Damo. He has been with his little canine friend "Gypsy" most of her life. The two are inseparable. I thought I'd pass onto you what he said about her, especially in the light of your beautiful comments about consolation.

"You can't explain the bond you have with a dog when you're homeless. You've got to be there to understand it. It's why I'm on the streets. If I went to a hostel, no dogs are allowed. Do you think I'm going to give her up just so I can sleep in a warm bed? No chance. It doesn't work like that. I'd rather sleep on cardboard and cuddle up to her."

When I wrote my Christmas novel, *King of Hearts*, I had an entire section in Act 2 in which my main character, Jake, is homeless on the streets after having lost a fortune in poker tournaments in Casino City. He is being hunted by a mobster called the Undertaker. It's bleak midwinter. Jake is freezing outside on a backstreet pavement, trying to get warm in an old sleeping bag. Suddenly he feels a wet nose on his face. A German shepherd is trying to slip inside his sleeping bag. He lets her. The two become one. The dog, whom Jake calls Sandy (after a girl who also kept him warm in the night), goes everywhere with him. You'll have to read it to see what happens.

I come back to our topic. Is it logical that the source of so much of our consolation in this life will be absent from the life to come? It is inconceivable to me that if heaven is perfect then dogs like Gypsy will be absent. We know that our loving Heavenly Father will judge us on the last day. One of the things that Jesus will ask us is whether we fed the hungry, clothed the naked, visited the prisoner etc. He makes it clear that in visiting the most vulnerable, *we are visiting Him*! If that's the case, and dogs minister to the needs of the homeless, then they are also ministering to Him! Those who minister to the homeless will be in heaven. Ergo . . . dogs are in heaven!

There is a curious and poignant detail in the parable Jesus narrated about the homeless man Lazarus. Jesus says that the rich man inside his palatial home was eating with his five brothers. Now I'm no mathematician but I do know that 1 (the rich man) plus 5 (his brothers) makes 6. There is a number in Judaism, as you know, that connotes and symbolizes perfection. It's the number 7. If the six brothers feasting inside had acknowledged that the seventh man starving outside had been their brother, including him within their circle would have completed and perfected their number. But they do not. While Jesus regards Lazarus as his brother, they fail to recognize him.

So, I come back time and time again to this idea of perfection. It is impossible to conceive of anything more perfect than heaven. If we can imagine something more perfect, then it cannot be said to be heaven. If imagining heaven without dogs renders the concept of heaven imperfect, then we have not imagined heaven, at least not according to biblical standards. With that in mind, I'll leave us with a quote from the late great Dr Billy Graham. It was in response to someone who asked him if their dog would be in heaven. He replied,

"God will prepare everything for our **perfect** happiness in Heaven, and if it takes my dog being there, I believe he'll be there."

Sophie will be there. Chester too. And countless men and women served by Betel. As well as those faultless canine friends served by Dogs on the Streets.

Love,

Mark.

Dear Mark,

The idea of the *perfection* of heaven is an intriguing one. Billy Graham (again): "Heaven will be the perfection we have always longed for." He goes on to say, "All the things that made earth unlovely and tragic will be absent in heaven." Is it therefore fair to extrapolate that all the things that made earth *lovely* and *joyful* will be *present* in heaven?

As with heaven, we can understand perfection as a concept, but it is impossible for us to comprehend as a reality because we are imperfect. For all the merits of our argument that heaven could not be heaven without our dogs, I believe that there is a "how much more" to this hope that we have. As you have said previously, as we will be transformed, so, indeed, will they. I believe that we have only had a foretaste here on earth of the love, companionship and joy that will be ours, with our dogs, in heaven.

And to any who would think all this rather fanciful, C.S. Lewis (again) writes, "A continual looking forward to the eternal world is not a form of escapism or wishful thinking, but one of the things a Christian is meant to do." Though, in this life, we will never be able to comprehend what awaits us, we can imagine and hope, inspired by the creativity of the inspiration of the Holy Spirit – the same imagination, hope, and inspiration that allows us to create.

Of course, the definition of the "perfection we have always longed for" will differ from person to person. There may be some who would consider the presence of dogs in heaven something that would make it less than the perfection they have longed for. So, can we argue for the presence of our dogs in heaven purely on the basis that heaven would not be perfect *for us* if our dogs were not to be there?

I believe that, in our emails after the loss of Sophie, I tried to explain that it felt as though something of *myself* had been lost – a part of me. I think that is more a truth than just a feeling. If I am to be perfected and complete in heaven's perfection, my wholeness will include her – however and whatever that looks like.

I am leaning towards the theory that our dogs will be in heaven because of who they have been to us, because they have been part of us. They have been instruments of grace to us – adding to us – contributing to our Christlikeness and our own perfection. They are, so very much, what makes us who we are.

They will be there because we will be there.

I am saving *King of Hearts* until Christmas!

Nev.

16

Vegetarian Lions

Dear Nev,

These are great points. I have often wondered about whether heaven would be perceived as perfect by someone who had been bitten and terrified by a dog when they were a child, to take one example. I agree that heaven, from the point of view of a dog-traumatized human soul, would be regarded as imperfect if it contained dogs. But then all of us, I'm sure, would take the same view of lions and snakes. In their unredeemed form – i.e., as they are now in the natural world – they are dangerous. I would not want to head off on foot on a heavenly safari where the lions were still maneaters and where the king cobras still spat lethal venom into our eyes!

And this is where your point about perfection meaning *transformation* is surely so important and right. The prophet Isaiah prophecies that in the future paradise the lion will lie down with the lamb, and the little child will play with the snake. Presumably this means that these animal creatures have, like us, undergone a radical and divine metamorphosis to make them able to inhabit the new heaven and earth. The lion has become vegetarian, and the snake has become harmless (maybe even, subversively, a healer). Heaven, to be perfect, must be safe. The child must be safe from all predators, including human ones, and the lamb must be safe from being slaughtered.

This also helps me to navigate my way past a point of disagreement. I don't know that I can agree that only those dogs/ animals that have interacted with loving humans are destined for heaven, by virtue of their interaction with souled beings like us. I want to believe that, but then I think of all the dogs that have had no interaction with loving humans, either because no humans are around, or because they are being mistreated by callous and cruel people. To be a just and fair Father, God must have a place in his new creation for them too – for those canines that Richard Adams called "the plague dogs."

I don't think interaction with loving humans can be the only criterion, therefore – as if our dogs get carried with us in the transporter beam to heaven (excuse the Star Trek analogy!). I believe that every aspect of the natural world – which in this iteration we have often so foolishly abused – will be redeemed and renewed. It is in this renewal that I find hope. When the Holy Scriptures speak about a "new heaven" and a "new earth", the Greek word does not mean *new* in a chronological sense (as in a brand-new heaven/earth *replacing* the old). It means new in a qualitative sense – a heaven and earth created from the old, and therefore still recognizable, albeit perfected.

Therefore, all dogs, lions, cats, lambs, snakes etc will be recognizably the same creatures but renewed, metamorphosized, resurrected, redeemed, glorified, incorruptible, etc. They will be seen as part of the perfection of heaven even by those who have been harmed by them. Why? Because they will be rendered safe, tame, loving. They will be restored to the original Edenic blueprint. In other words, they will be our FRIENDS – something of which we have a foretaste now when we walk in the fells with our dogs, talking with them in a way we would never talk to someone else.

Is this not a beautiful dream, a stunning prospect?

I have recently been blessed with my first grandchild (one of the deepest joys of my life) and he, like his father (my oldest), is obsessed with dinosaurs! This cannot be a harking back to the mists of a distant ancient era because humans and dinosaurs never interacted. Maybe it's a harking forward! To the new earth when God's children will play with real dinosaurs, ones that have been tamed and perfected by the divine love. Maybe the euphoric glee that pours out of children when they clutch a plastic T Rex and imagine it growling is evidence that one day, in the new creation, we will not so much be homo sapiens as homo *ludens* (those who play!).

This is very interesting, stimulating, and thought provoking.

Thank you for your friendship and for this discussion.

Love,

Mark.

Dear Mark,

Please feel free to continue to use as many *Star Trek* analogies as required! I am a great fan of all the various generations and series. The most recent *Picard* on Amazon is, possibly, their deepest and most engaging yet.

To clarify: I am not saying that interaction with loving humans or, indeed, loving interaction with humans is the *only* criterion for the existence of animals in heaven. I offer the theory as an additional (and pastoral) argument for their place with us in eternity, but not the only one. After all, when the question "Do dogs go to heaven?" is asked, it is surely influenced by the desire for our pets to be part of our eternal existence. For me, I'm not sure if heaven's perfection will be lessened if it is missing the odd cow; my deepest concern is for those with whom I have shared my life here.

This leads me to consider how very different each person's idea of perfection may be. However unfathomable it may seem to us, there are some people who just don't like dogs very much, but not because of a fear or a bad experience. I am also acutely aware of the fact that, for a significant amount of people, my own presence there would mean that heaven would be less than perfect for them. This calls forth the necessity of *transformation* for perfection to be possible – that place of no fear, no pain, and where the only tears will be ones of joy. In fact, however much we might have our own ideas of what perfection will be, there really is/will be only one perfection in truth, and we all will see it as such when we are there.

I, too, am excited at the prospect of *renewal* as opposed to replacement. I have so many places still to explore, and so many walks I would have wished to have completed prior to my knees somewhat limiting those ambitions. I believe that the *new* earth will be recognisable to us even in its transformation, and available for us to continue to explore but with a supernatural body – how great does that sound? In the joy of such unrestricted exploration, rather than trying to overcome the pain of arthritis, my soul will be released to be able to cry "holy, holy, holy" in unison with the rest of the (re)new(ed) creation with which I will also have a renewed friendship.

I, too, am now experiencing the joy of a first grandchild. Little Nancy is now 8 months old. The joy, for me, is in the bond that goes beyond blood relation. Whereas there was always a missing element in the relationship I had with my stepchildren, because I am not their father, that missing piece is not so pronounced in the relationship between grandparent and grandchild. I delight in the way in which she ignores everyone else in the room (including her Nanny Lesley) when I am with her! I believe there will be a special bond between us.

On your final thought, I am rereading Henri Nouwen's *Genesee Diary* – an account of his eight months in a Trappist Monastery. In one of the first entries, he recounts the Abbot, John Eudes, explaining to him, "The sole idea of the monastic life is that of creating a lifelong vacation!" It is a wonderful attitude, and one that would be so far removed from most people's idea of monastic life. Yet, I have tasted something of that in this last couple of years here in Eden. In the separation of removing ourselves to north Cumbria and living in the freedom of being able to concentrate on God without distraction, and to live each day as the Holy Spirit inspires unto purity, creativity, and rest, it feels as if there has been something 'monastic' in that lifestyle. It feels like vacation. It feels as if 'play' is very much on the Father's agenda for our perfection.

Yet, I am getting a sense that this time will soon be coming to an end. The challenge will be to carry that same sense of freedom into whatever and wherever the Father will lead us next.

With much love, my friend,

Nev.

Beam Me Up

Dear Nev,

Thank you so much for giving your blessing for *Star Trek* references. You may know that the only series to regularly feature a dog is *Star Trek: Enterprise*. Captain Archer has an American Beagle called Porthos. Archer's dog travelled with him throughout his adventures as captain, going boldly where no dog has gone before (this line is used of him in the episode *Strange New World*). It's worth watching just for the dog. He's gorgeous. He came from a litter of four puppies all named after the musketeers of Dumas's famous novel. A Ferengi appropriately named Muk calls him "a lower life form." Porthos is one of only four characters who appears in all the seasons.

Anyway, enough of *Star Trek*, except perhaps to say this. I mentioned the transporter in my last email to you, and of course the most famous expression associated with that device is Captain Kirk's refrain, "Beam me up, Scotty." This has prompted me to make two points before we continue our discussions about dogs in heaven. The first is to remind each other of what we already know that heaven is not somewhere "up there" to which souls will ascend after death. This is a very common myth, believed by many Christians too. But Jesus taught the opposite. In His teaching two thousand years ago, he said that the kingdom of heaven comes down to where we are.

If I'm honest, I'm not sure about all this up/down language that we commonly use. It's often taken very literally, but I suspect that we will come to learn that these prepositions were never meant to be taken at face value but rather point to ideas about what lies "beyond" – ideas not easily rendered in finite human language. Nevertheless, I'll use them just for the sake of brevity and say again that the Father's plan has never been to bring us up to heaven (in a Beam Me Up kind of way) but rather to bring heaven down to where we are. As I've often written over the years, "Jesus came to bring heaven to those who are experiencing hell on earth." That's our task too.

In my imagination, heaven is not some realm up there (wherever "there" is) where we sit on clouds like portly Victorian babies and pluck harps for eternity. I can't think of anything worse. Rather, it's the new heaven and new earth in which we will one day live and laugh. I believe the Bible is consistent about this. One day, the entire cosmos will be made new, and the city of gold will descend to bless the purified and beautified landscape of the new creation. Far from souls ascending to heaven, heaven is going to come to earth. It will be quite literally heaven on earth. And we will enjoy it in glorified, resurrected, perfected bodies.

The second point is this: the focus of heaven will not be our dogs but God. This is obvious but it's worth repeating. Heaven may be described as a place, yes, but ultimately it's a person. Or more accurately three persons – the Father, the Son, and the Holy Spirit. In this earthly life, and in our mortal bodies, we know this Trinity of Love only by faith. When heaven comes to earth, we will know the Three-in-One by sight. We will see Him face to face. Our connection with Him will be immediate, not mediated as it is in this life by the Holy Spirit. When heaven comes to earth, it will be all about Him. He will wipe away our tears. We will enjoy the ultimacy of intimacy.

What has this got to do with dogs? Everything. When we ask, "Do dogs go to heaven?", we are asking the wrong question. The real question is, "Will dogs be part of the new creation?" I think, as you do, the answer is yes. But will our eyes be always drawn to them? I think not. The Bible teaches that we are going to enjoy the immediacy of the Father's love forever. It will be His presence on which our hearts and eyes will be trained. Our dogs will wonder at Him too, as the animals do when they meet Aslan in Narnia. We will all be preoccupied with this great, great Father. I believe – as in your dream – they will adore their Heavenly Master, just as they have us!

So, maybe the *Star Trek* analogies should be handled with care! I believe that dogs will be a part of the new creation, and other animals too. Will all animals enjoy the new earth? I think the answer must be yes. All animals were a part of the Garden of Eden, looked after in love by Adam and Eve. Every species was rescued by Noah on the Ark. Whether these stories are meant to be interpreted metaphorically or literally, the message is simple and easily understandable: nature in its entirety will be rescued and redeemed when heaven comes to earth in all its fullness. This will include every creature, not just our dogs. Cats will enjoy the new creation too.

But here's the point: we won't, I suspect, be as doting with them as we are now. Our focus will be on God, not dogs. And maybe this gives some comfort to those who are indifferent to or scared by dogs in this life. If in the new earth we only have eyes for Him, then we shan't be distracted or disconcerted by animals, who in any event will be renewed in such a way as to put all at their ease. We will have the same reaction to the heavenly landscapes that we love to explore, only our first love will not be for the created but for the Creator, with whom we will walk and talk as

Adam and Eve once did.

So, this email probably marks the last of my Star Trek allusions!

It was fun while it lasted.

Love and blessings to you both, especially as you sense the winds of change,

Mark.

Dear Mark,

Firstly, yes and Amen to all you have said here. I believe that it would be important for these points to be stated up front in any serious discussion about the presence of our dogs in heaven. This understanding that our whole focus will be God, and that the new heaven and new earth will be all about Him is, possibly, the main reason behind the condescending laughter of the religious to my childhood hopes of having my dog alongside me for eternity. They think that it won't matter to me once I am there. I remember being rather worried that heaven would just be one long, eternal worship service and, of course, in a way it will be, but I now understand that worship can take many different forms, while always fixing our eyes on Him. Much of the discipline of living life in the Spirit is learning to worship in all things, all circumstances, every situation, and every activity, seeing God in everyone and everything. I believe, as we learn to do this, we are closer to 'seeing' the Kingdom of heaven which is 'upon' us. As you say, in the eternity of the new heaven and earth we will see Him without the mediation of the Spirit, for the new heaven and earth will be *Him*. We will see Him in everything – all things, including each other.

I agree that the Beam Me Up theology of heaven is flawed yet, in some ways, it is understandable. Jesus did, after all, ascend out of the sight of the disciples. I think that it is natural to think of heaven as the opposite to the underworld and, if the underworld is somewhere beneath, then heaven should be somewhere above. The heavenly city descends upon the new earth, and that's the point isn't it? I was only talking with Lesley about this a couple of days ago when I surprised her by saying that we were not going to heaven!

Whatever happens to our souls in the meantime, we will live out eternity physically (though with a 'spiritual' body – whatever that means) in the new earth, with heaven somehow amongst us. Even as I write that, I realise how close that is to the life we should be living already, except that, in eternity, this beautiful earth will be renewed, and heaven will be in plain sight amongst us. The difficulty we have, of course, is that our mind's eye has not seen what the Father has in store for us – we just don't have the ability to be able to comprehend what it will truly be like to live in His constant and immediate presence 'beyond the veil'.

So, with our whole focus being on God in eternity, will it matter to us whether our dogs are there with us?

Our understanding of the Trinity is that each person perfectly loves, and is perfectly loved by, the other persons. Yet, God created the world, and us, to be objects of His love. Somehow, His capacity to love goes beyond perfection. Why resurrect us into a new creation if we are not to love it and care for it while, at the same time, be fully focussed on loving and worshipping God? Loving and caring for the new creation will be another expression of loving and worshipping Him.

I think that I might dote on Sophie even more than I have here, for doting on her will be an expression of doting on Him. Being *like* Him surely means a much greater capacity to love.

Your Noah reference reminds me of an amusing cartoon I saw recently.

The picture was of the ark floating on the water. The caption read:

Day 48. From within the ark a voice is heard, "Hey guys, you won't believe how tasty this unicorn is!"

From the sublime to the ridiculous.

Nev

18

Joy Bringers

Hi Nev,

I love the unicorn gag. Brilliant. Although, if this conversation is ever shared more widely, I fear you may have just offended an army of young unicorn lovers! And I love also what you write about the both-and nature of our future heavenly existence. Perhaps we should draw a distinction here between our primary and secondary orders of joy in the new earth. The primary joy will surely be the fact that we will constantly enjoy the Threefold God forever and ever just for who they are. Our focus will be on the three persons of the Trinity in the beauty of their holiness. At the same time, I believe we will be constantly in awe at the matchless genius of the new heaven and earth.

This of course includes redeemed and renewed animal creation. This will fill us with joy too, albeit at a secondary order. Just as when, in this life, we are filled with wonder by looking at the devotion of our dogs, the effortlessness of an eagle in flight, and the stubborn durability of a mountain, and just as these things lead many into a joyful "thank you" to our loving Father, so when we are living in the new earth our eyes will constantly be wide open with wonder at "the shock of the new," to use a phrase I once heard in relation to art. In all these things, it will be the joy of what we see that inspires our delight in the joy-giver.

And that brings me to my one thought for today! For what is it that our dogs bring to our lives if it isn't joy? I know that dogs, like cats, have a very important healing and de-stressing effect too. But it is the joy factor I want to emphasize because it is something that I believe loving our animals causes us to experience time and again. They simply make us smile, often laugh. And we all know what the Good Book says about a cheerful heart being good medicine. The joy of seeing our dogs doing something funny, something adorable, always fills me with gratitude and brings me a little more out of myself.

I remember when I was training for ordained ministry being tasked to do a very tough one-year placement at a hospice for the dying in Nottingham. I went week after week and sat by bedsides trying to talk with weary, ashen, dying patients. I bathed them and washed them. I helped make their beds. I remember not being able to get through to them at all. Then, one day, I asked if I could take my Black Lab Mij with me – the Lab who saved my life from the bull. She and I went everywhere during my training, except the hospice. The people running the place said yes. So, the next week I took her in on a lead.

I cannot begin to describe the difference it made. When I drew up alongside a patient, their grey faces were suddenly filled with colour and their sad eyes with joy. They came alive in front of me. "What's her name?" "Isn't she beautiful?" "May I stroke her?" Mij was so sweet with them. As I finished talking with one, another on the ward would shout, "Over here! Bring her here!" She continued to bring joy every time we went. Today I'm sure this sort of animal therapy is very common, but in the 1980s I had never heard of such a thing. I merely responded to a holy instinct. Mij was like an angel. Albeit one with fur.

That's really all I have to say. I believe heaven will be filled with moments of wonder and joy like this, when the sheer beauty and brilliance of the Creator as we watch His redeemed creatures will fill us with even more joy, and a greater compulsion to give Him thanks, to give Him our praise.

Who knows what things we will see? We can only imagine. But I am sure that what we see of our dogs in heaven will not lead us to obsess and focus on them but will draw our hearts out to even more passionate overtures of love for the Joy Bringer.

With love and blessings,

Mark.

Dear Mark,

This is beautiful. Clearly, with Holy Spirit inspiration, you pioneered the use of animals to bring solace and comfort, even healing, to those most in need. Once again, it shows how our dogs reflect Jesus' example of how we should care for each other. In as much as angels are messengers of God, surely Mij proved to be not only the Father's messenger for those in the hospice, but to all of us that we should heed her example.

Sophie was probably our pub's greatest asset. Families from faraway places would make sure that they returned to us, year after year, just to meet her again. There was one family with a young boy who had very challenging behavioural difficulties – probably ADHD and other learning and social disabilities. They returned to us as often as possible because, according to them, our pub was the only place they could come as a family where the boy would be calm, content and at ease. He would spend hours with Sophie, as she gently rolled her ball towards him and caught it again, as he threw it back to her, albeit weakly and with little dexterity. If this had been anyone else, she would have given up and tried another person who could have given her a better game, but she ignored everyone else to give this boy her attention. She was so gentle and understanding of his inabilities. As the ball looped up, often in completely the wrong direction, she would catch it and roll it back to him with such patience. With every catch of the ball that Sophie made, the boy would cry out in delight, jumping with joy on the spot, his body trembling with excitement. Many times, I watched this game with tears in my eyes, as did his parents. We had other children with similar difficulties come to the pub over the years and, with each one, Sophie always exhibited an unusual gentleness, sympathy and understanding – quite remarkable.

Our Father's desire is for our joy to be complete. Jesus tells us this. Whether, in eternity, there will be *levels* of joy, I don't know, but we do know that our joy will be complete.

We have no idea or comprehension of what that will feel like, or look like, except for the glimpses of joy we have experienced here in this life – often, as you say, through our pets. Julian of Norwich's "All shall be well, and all shall be well, and all manner of thing shall be well" perhaps best sums up the completeness of joy that will be ours. Our joy will be His and His joy will be ours. The consolation that our dogs have provided for us in this life will be transformed, consumed, and perfected by this joy. Our relationship with them will no longer bear this element of consolation – for we will lack nothing – but will be replaced with rejoicing together in the glorious presence of Father, Son, and Holy Spirit. Together, along with the rest of the new creation, our focus and our joy will be in Him.

*I can only imagine what it will be like when I walk by Your side.
I can only imagine what my eyes will see when Your face is
before me;
I can only imagine
I can only imagine when that day comes and I find myself
standing in the Son.
I can only imagine when all I will do is forever, forever worship You;
I can only imagine.*

(Bart Millard)

One of my favourite songs!

Nev.

19

The Very Dear One

Dear Nev,

Your reminiscences about Sophie really touched me. I'll never forget when you and Lesley ran the Farquharson Arms in Pimperne. One of the times I visited, I very vividly recall Sophie wandering around the tables and saying hello to all the regulars and visitors. I've never seen anyone do Pub Church better than you three – Nev, Lesley, and Sophie. What a Trinity! Those days were very memorable to me. Do you remember when one of the members of your congregation linked me up with C.S. Lewis's stepson, Douglas Gresham? A few months later my youngest Sam and I found ourselves visiting Malta and having dinner with him. Sam was overjoyed to wield the original swords from the Narnia movies.

I'll also never forget you telling me what the translation was of your pub's name. The Son of the Very Dear One. It always struck me as the perfect pub name for someone who so clearly has been gripped by the revelation of the Father's love. I'm sure you remember me quoting one of my favourite authors – Father Brennan Manning – talking about the big question people used to be asked over 150 years ago. Not "Have you been born again?" (the question most contemporary evangelicals ask). But rather, "Has your heart been seized by the power of a great affection?" That's the secret of life right there! Your pub was a thin place – a place where strangers were able to have their hearts captivated by the love of the Very Dear One. And Sophie was such an indispensable part of this I cannot think of the pub without her. The Arms were inseparable from her paws!

I think dogs should play a much greater part in church life. After all, when I was ministering as an ordained person, I wore a dog collar! I remember reading an excellent book about Cat and Dog theology too. The difference between cats and dogs is that dogs have masters and cats have staff! I used several of my Black Labs over the years in my sermons especially when I was talking to children at family services about obeying their Master, Jesus. My dogs would always illustrate the point faultlessly. Never work with children or animals they say.

Rubbish!

Cherith was telling me yesterday about the next phase of training for staff at her special school. It's called PACK TYPES. It sounds inspiring. It uses the analogy of dogs. The various species illustrate your unique personality type. It's a whole new psychometric test and it's all the rage in education, business, the NHS, everywhere. Dogs are being used to help us understand the way we are and the way we relate to each other at work and home – both actually and aspirationally. Once again, we see how dogs are key to our wellbeing in so many aspects of life. They cannot just be the product of evolution or human engineering. They are a GIFT from the Very Dear One!

As we learn how important dogs are in this old earth, how can they not be important in the age to come? The new earth will surely be populated by redeemed animals. The great story of the Bible begins and ends in a garden. It begins in the Garden of

Eden with human beings tasked to name the animals and to look after them with the same rule of love that the Very Dear One has been demonstrating. It ends with paradise — a word that means heavenly garden. Just as the first garden had animals, so surely this last one will too. Bella is never happier than when she finds herself in a big garden. She comes alive in a way that's unique. Maybe she's having an instinct of what's to come.

I am thoroughly loving this interchange of emails. I love especially the quote you included at the end of your last message of that great song "I can only imagine." I will never forget my son Phil singing that at the funeral of a man who was like a grandfather to my kids when I was vicar of St Andrew's. As he sang about imagining the glory of our eternal future, we were all energised with hope even as the tears of sadness fell. How does anyone manage to live through grief without faith in in the glorious and great beyond — a beyond in which we will meet Mij and Sophie, Chester and Molly, and all the others again?

We all should try to imagine heaven, to picture our dogs greeting us in the garden, their tails wagging furiously.

Then leading us to the true focus of heaven — the Very Dear One.

Love to you both,

Mark.

Dear Mark,

To continue where you left off: this correspondence is really our *imaginings*. Informed imaginings they may be, coloured by our hopes, but imaginings, nevertheless. It is worth repeating that, though many would see a futility in what we are considering, it is a worthwhile journey; for to have faith, there needs to be hope. For there to be hope, we must have something to hope for – something on which to base the reality of the yet unseen. Heaven's perfection is beyond our comprehension but, at least, we can comprehend the very best that we can imagine, and then use that as our reference point from which to believe that heaven will be even better. We have already stated many times that, for people like us, the best we can imagine would have to include dogs. It would have to include animals, and a friendship between us and them. It would have to include beauty as well as glory. What we can conclude is that our eternity will be all those things and more, much more – infinitely better.

When we were last walking together here in the Lakes, Lesley referred to me as 'The Old Man of the Fells.' Your photo of me, which you entitled 'The Old Man filling the fells with laughter,' reminds me of your earlier comments on the importance of laughter in friendship. I realise that, for all my own imaginings of heaven, often the idea that it will be the most tremendous fun has somehow escaped me. Yet, it will be more fun than we have ever experienced before. We will laugh like never before. With regards to eternity, too often we concentrate on the absence of tears and pain, and not enough on the presence of the belly laugh – the laughter I can see in the photo you took of me when we walked together!

Back to dogs. We have both recognised the way in which the Father has used dogs in such a wonderful way to teach us so many important things about who He is, who we are, and how we should live – the *Pack Types* tests being the latest example of that. We also spoke, yesterday, of the thrill of uncovering and discovering the clues that the Father and the Son and the Holy

Spirit have left us both in His Word and in the world around us. Eternity will be a never-ending life of discovery of God. Yes, we will see Him as He is, and we will know Him more intimately than ever before but, I believe, the process will continue, as there will always be something more to learn and experience of the Infinite One. I wonder: as they have been on earth, will dogs continue in their role as our guides in the 'more than' of heaven? Not as intermediaries, of course, but as 'Pointers' (see what I did there?) to the glory of the Holy One in our eternal voyage of discovery and worship.

Love to the three of you,

Nev.

20

A Fishy Heaven

My dear Nev,

There's so much in your last email that I agree with and that I want to explore further. I'll leave the subject of beauty (one which has always fascinated me) until another time. I'll just respond to your comments about imagining heaven. I don't know whether it's because we're in the Lake District on holiday right now, but the Romantic poets have been on my mind. One of them, P.B. Shelley, wrote about the imagination. He described it as "synthetic". Synthesis means joining two things together in a way that surprises and delights. An example would be when the poet Ted Hughes likens a thistle to "a grasped fistful of splintered weapons." A brilliant synthesis!

All our imaginings of heaven must involve at least a little bit of synthetic thinking. Two days ago, while we were walking with you and Lesley in the driving rain at Rydal Water (what a treat that was), I took five photos of Bella running along the edge of the lake in ever increasing amounts of speed and joy. They're a stunning sequence, with the drenched hills and mountains in the background. Scenes like these fill our memories and are recorded as the best of our moments. When we imagine heaven, which must be the perfect and non-temporal experience of such moments in time, we inevitably synthesize – we are drawn to say that heaven must be like this, only better.

Maybe it's because we've been driving past some of the most glorious rivers in Britain, but I've been thinking a lot about my trout fishing days as a boy. My adoptive dad taught me how to fish. We would head down with our rods to the river with our chunky Black Labrador called Bronte, named after Nelson, who was Viscount Bronte. I have many memories of this — some not so happy, as when I was devoured by midges while trying to fish for trout in North West Scotland. That said, fishing for trout was for the most part a heavenly experience. I remember one time seeing a kingfisher. I could not imagine a more finely and strikingly coloured bird. They'll be in heaven too.

When I later studied literature, I came across a poem by Rupert Brooke. It was simply called 'Heaven.' In it, Brooke imagined a trout in its liquid world speculating about what lay above and beyond. Some people say it's satirical, but I think it's more complicated than this — even though Brooke mentions a "fishy heaven" (you could argue "fishy" means suspect here!). Brooke's poetry veered towards the sentimental more than the satirical. I think there was at least a part of Brooke's heart that hoped that what the trout was speculating about might have a human equivalent. Here's the trout's creed:

Somewhere, beyond Space and Time,
Is wetter water, slimier slime!
And there (they trust) there swimmeth One
Who swam ere rivers were begun,
Immense, of fishy form and mind,
Squamous, omnipotent, and kind;
And under that Almighty Fin,
The littlest fish may enter in

These lines are frivolous, but there's something quite enchanting about them too. Here's some more:

Oh! never fly conceals a hook,
Fish say, in the Eternal Brook,
But more than mundane weeds are there,
And mud, celestially fair;
Fat caterpillars drift around,
And Paradisal grubs are found;
Unfading moths, immortal flies,
And the worm that never dies.
And in that Heaven of all their wish,
There shall be no more land, say fish.

I love the way Brooke imagines heaven from a trout's point of view. It's like the best that a trout experiences in this old earth, only more perfect – more perfect weeds, mud, caterpillars, grubs that are paradisal, moths that are unfading, flies that are immortal, worms that never die. In this perfect world, there will be no concealed hooks and, better still for the trout, no LAND!

Wonderful!

This is a great example of synthesis. Heaven is going to be like the best that this earth has to offer, only better! And I'm sure that this expresses, under all the wit and whimsy, the poet's own longings. After all, he nods to his own surname in the capitalized expression, "Eternal Brook."

I could go on.

Maybe next time I'll reflect on the idea of beauty from a spiritual perspective. Theology over the centuries has been far too preoccupied with truth and not enough with beauty. Maybe I'll ramble about the word 'wish' in the penultimate line of Brooke's poem about heaven (*desire* is one of the strongest arguments for the existence of heaven). But for now, I end with a question: what would heaven look like from Sophie's point of view?

From Bella's? From Chester's? From Mij's? Do you have some 'imaginings' in response?

Much love to you both,

Mark.

Dear Mark,

Brooke's poem of the trout's view of heaven is marvellous. To sum it up; it would be all that it enjoys, but more so, and nothing of that which it doesn't! On one of our trips together, Guy and I were taken to the Villa Rufolo in Ravello, high up on the Amalfi coast of Italy. The gardens overlooked the spectacular coast, and within the gardens was a fishpond which, to our eyes, seemed to contain just one, very contented goldfish. The goldfish enjoyed the most beautiful pond and, if it could consider heaven at all, would have probably thought it was already there (provided, of course, it was an introvert). Yet just one leap out of the water would have revealed the great expanse of the Mediterranean Sea and the astounding view of the coast of which it was blissfully unaware. Our imaginings can only take us so far; there is a huge expanse of infinity way beyond all that we could think of or even begin to understand, yet it is there, just beyond our pond.

My first thought of what heaven would be like for Sophie was one containing a never-ending game of chasing after a ball with the limitless energy of her transformed and spiritual body, and the eternal patience (and endurance) of the most excellent Ball Thrower. I then remembered reading somewhere that a Collie's fascination with a ball stems from the fact that the game triggers the same endorphins they experience when herding sheep.

Both activities require expert visual ability and concentration, together with lightning reflexes and physical dexterity. It is interesting that they are designed to enjoy doing what they were made for. Sophie never had to work on a sheep farm and had never experienced the thrill of what she was made to do, but still had a clear idea of what she enjoyed. She just didn't understand why she enjoyed it so much. Sophie's idea of heaven would be flawed, because of her lack of understanding as to why she loved the things that she did. Perhaps, even with her obvious joy and sense of security in the fact that I was her master, this only pointed to a greater reality and a time when she will enjoy being perfectly loved and mastered by her Creator.

The things we love, desire, and hope for, those things we enjoy or consider beautiful, may just be a taste — perhaps even a symptom — of what we shall be when we are perfected in Him for eternity, when our true identities will be finally revealed. The love that you and I have for our dogs may be just that — a love for dogs — or is it a taste of a greater expression of love for which we have no understanding yet? What we do know is that all our loves, desires, hopes, and dreams will be consummated in Him.

This is joy beyond all we could imagine.

Love,

Nev.

21

Molly's Tale

Dear Nev,

Your thoughts about Sophie caused me to wake early with thoughts about Molly, the Black Lab I had before Bella. I know you remember meeting her when I was vicar of St Andrew's. She and I were inseparable. She came to every staff meeting with me and lay at my feet while I chaired the meetings in the chapel. She was very used to being in sacred spaces and among the best of people, yourself included. She was a very special friend.

I have never told anyone what happened to her. When I fell on hard times in 2012, my estate agent came to me to say the landlord wanted Molly out of the flat I was renting. I was devastated. I wrote to my sister-in-law. She then sent an S.O.S to her friends in Suffolk to see if anyone could give Molly a new home. A lovely lady called Jane replied. She and I started corresponding. She told a remarkable story. It was November when we made contact.

In July of that same year (2012), Jane had been walking with her Black Labrador in the woods when an adder struck. Her dog died and she was utterly devastated. As we talked, an extraordinary set of "coincidences" started to emerge. Her Black Lab had been called Molly. Hers was the same age as my Molly, almost to the day. If ever there seemed to be a sense of providential synchronicity, this was it.

The very sad day came when Cherith and I travelled to Suffolk to hand Molly over to Jane. I won't try to describe what it's like having to give up a dog for adoption. I'm adopted, and I can't even begin to imagine what my birth mother (who I met for the first, and last, time last year) went through handing Claire and me to the nuns in Hackney. Cherith and I were forever scarred by the experience. Enough said!

In the weeks that followed, Jane very kindly sent me emails and photographs of Molly in her new home – acres of farmland in Suffolk (a truly beautiful county) and their second home in Scotland. Molly had really landed on her four pampered paws! She had new friends – canine and human – and the most glorious landscapes in which to roam and play. It filled my heart with such joy amidst the tears. Here's one of Jane's emails:

"Molly has been here four weeks now and she has really settled. She has got into the routine; she is eating well, and everybody loves her. She is out on the yard with us every day and comes round the fields to do the horses, collecting sticks as she goes. She has been to our holiday cottage in Scotland and just loved it. It is right on the beach and as you already know, she loves water, so she was in her element. We took her ball, and she spent hours chasing it on the beach. Strangely, she always had to return with it via the water! She is an absolute delight, and we all love her. I'm sure you are missing her but thank you so much for giving her to us. I hope this reassures you that she is happy."

It did reassure us, and so did the photos. Molly was happier than she could ever have been with me in my first-floor flat with no garden, stuck indoors for much of the day while I tried to scratch out a living at my desk as a writer. She was in heaven on earth. I simply cannot imagine anything more perfect for my beloved and faithful friend. It made the letting go much easier knowing she was so happy and free.

I find it helpful to think of this story — one which I have never been able to tell before — when I think of our dogs in the afterlife. Some dogs are blessed enough to enjoy a taste of that now, as we do when our loving Heavenly Father gives us a teaser of the everlasting fun and freedom of heaven in our sometimes mundane and sorrowful present. Molly was one such lucky dog.

I was sorrowful this morning when I reread the correspondence about Molly. Bella must have sensed it. She made her way to my side of the bed, hopped up, and rested her head in my left hand, her chin in my palm. She seemed to know that something was amiss and that I needed to be consoled (there's that beautiful word again). They really do love us, don't they? No wonder Oprah Winfrey said,

"Over the years, I have felt that the truest, purest love — the love of God, really (I imagine that's what God's love feels like) — is the love that comes from your dog."

Amen.

Dear Mark,

I was deeply moved by your email as I read it first thing. I cannot imagine the wrench of having to give up your dog. The idea of giving up a child is beyond me as I have no children of my own. Perhaps, my capacity for paternal love was projected onto Sophie. Lesley would always explain to other people how close I was to Sophie, saying that she was my little girl. I would fight for her, protect her, and I have no doubt that I would have risked my life for her, had the need risen.

I was reminded of a day, walking back from the fells through a farmyard, when Sophie and I were surrounded by a pack of hunting hounds. These dogs were scraggy and feral; they had obviously been allowed to feed on a sheep carcass that lay to one side of the yard. There was no sign of anyone around to control them. As they approached and circled us, they tried to attack Sophie. The logical and sensible thing to do would have been to run – they weren't interested in me except that I was a hindrance to getting to Sophie. However, I was filled with an anger that I have rarely felt before or since and, roaring with rage, I swung my walking stick around my head (one with a dog's head handle rather like yours I believe) and went on the offensive while still holding Sophie on her lead behind me. I attacked any hound that came within reach with such ferocity that they soon started to back away. The hunters had become the hunted! We did not have to run for the gate – eventually, the beaten hounds decided to keep their distance, and allowed us to walk peacefully out of the yard. Only when I got back to the pub where I was staying did I begin to shake and realise what a dangerous predicament we had just experienced.

Beer helped.

I also remember the sense of panic that I used to feel whenever I couldn't find Sophie after we had a busy session at the pub, and she had been in the garden playing with anyone and everyone who would throw her ball for her. The thought of her being taken frightened me. So, I cannot imagine the pain of having to give her away. To know that Molly went to such a good home and enjoyed such a full life (the photos you shared are wonderful) is, indeed, consolation for both of you, but the loss of friendship remains.

I am so sorry, Mark.

It is that renewal and transformation of our friendship with our dogs in 'heaven' that excites me – a friendship which we have only tasted here. Sophie (and Chester) won't be substitutes for not being a father; they won't be the consolation, that they have been here, for loneliness and rejection; they will be true and everlasting friends. This morning, Bella gave you another glimpse of that friendship as she *cared* for you.

Earlier today, I weeded my potato patch with the help of the cows next door. As I was bent over, pulling up the weeds, I felt a prod in my lower back, and turned round to see four heifers, one of which was nudging me with her nose, almost playfully. As I tore up the weeds and grass, I passed them over the low wire fence for the cows to munch on. For all the grass in the huge field next door, it appears that the tufts of grass I was pulling up and giving to them, were far more delicious and preferable!

Friendship?

I like to think so.

It certainly cheered me as I think of my sister rapidly succumbing to cancer in hospital today – the consolation of our animal friends.

Love to you,

Nev.

22

A Dog Called Sprout

My Dear Nev,

Thank you so much for your kind words. And now I find myself needing to give the same to you. I am so sorry to hear about your sister. Truly. Cancer is one of the greatest of all evils. It destroys bodies and families. I have seen far too much of it among the people I care about in recent years. It has just taken my oldest friend, as you know. My neighbour Eleanor has been suffering from it for nearly twenty years. I see her walking past the window where my desk is. Sometimes she shuffles by with her two dogs whom she adores. It makes me sad every time to see the colour drained from her face. I am glad that she has two furry friends to keep her company.

Eighteen months ago, I heard that Eleanor had started writing poetry. The poems were coming out at a rush, and she was clearly being energised by them. When she told me she had enough for a book, I said I'd edit them for free and help her get them published, which she subsequently did with her husband Antony's help. As a birthday present for her, I arranged a surprise poetry reading for her in our local pub, The Cat and Custard Pot (a stone's throw from our front door). The place was busy that night. We all sipped local ale – the fruit of Kentish hops – while she sat on a bar stool in one corner and, with the help of a makeshift PA system, read her poems while we applauded.

Most of her poems are poignant laments about struggling all these years with her disease. They are incredibly powerful pieces. Always defiantly upbeat. Extremely insightful, with razor-sharp observations of the world, and especially of the glorious natural surroundings we both share. One of her poems is about the view from her house. On a clear and sunny day, you can see the white cliffs of Dover and, further away, the French coast. But then, when the sea mist sprawls inland, these vistas disappear. She wonders in her poem what the ancients thought as the distant horizon magically came and went. A bit like glimpses of heaven. Or whatever they called it.

Anyway, several of her poems are about dogs. The older of the two is called Sprout. Here's her tribute:

SPROUT

There's something about walking with a dog,
Everyone stops to talk to you!
I've just been for a stroll through Hythe
And have chatted to more folk in an hour
Than I normally do in a day.

Mind you, she is an unusually appealing dog -
Bright eyes, tiny black button nose, melting expression,
A cross between a Jack Russell and a Bichon Frise.
We thought that made her a Brussel
So, we called her Sprout.

When she was a puppy she was-smooth haired and tidy.
I wanted to name her Thistle,
But Antony wasn't having any of that.
Said it sounded too soft.
So, Sprout it was.

But her coat grew long and wild,
Sticking out in all directions,
More hair than fur.
Newly brushed she looks half presentable,
But within five minutes she's back to normal.

If you half close your eyes she looks like the business end
of a mop,
The old-fashioned string kind used by the caretaker at my
primary school.
Stick a pole up her bum and you could wash the floor with her.
I say we should have called her Scruffy,
Or maybe just Moppet.

What would we do without dogs, eh? They truly are our greatest friends and, like you say, we would do anything for them. Greater love hath no man than this, that he lay down his life for his (canine) friends. And not just canine, but other animals too. Eleanor has a poem about the cows in the field next door to her house. It's called 'Cows in the Garden'. They broke through the fence one time onto their property, 'churning up the grass with their hooves.' When she caught a movement in the garden out of the corner of her eye, she saw a cow with her young ruining their freshly mown lawn. "Oh bullocks!" she said. She would have loved what you wrote about cows.

I feel so much for people trapped in the cities, never seeing the countryside. I'm helping a guy write a book at the moment who worked in Medway STC – a prison for young offenders – for ten years. He became the enrichment manager there and organised trips into the countryside for the young people, most of whom had been gang members in London. He describes them sitting wide-eyed with wonder in fields, staring at cows and smelling grass soaked in rain for the very first time. People like you and me are so, so blessed. When we imagine heaven, we have the raw material of nature to inspire us. It is so unjust that people are robbed of this experience.

Anyway, say a prayer for Eleanor, as I will for your sister (please share her first name if you're allowed to).

With love to you and yours, especially your sister,

Mark.

Dear Mark,

Thank you again for your kind words and the offer to pray. My sister's name is Karen, though we all call her Kay. Eleanor sounds like a person I would instantly get on with – a dog lover with a very English sense of humour. I wonder how many nationalities would find 'sticking a pole up a dog's bum to turn it into a mop' funny. I certainly do.

Cancer may be one of the darkest mysteries of all. It is not just infirmity – it seems designed to torment. Like you (and most other people today), I am so tired of hearing about it, and seeing it around me. Death holds no sting for us, but cancer does. It withers, wastes, and eats away, while feeding itself. Father, give us gifts of healing for those who are suffering, as well as the grace to comfort and bring peace.

When we are walking in the Lakes, we often come across a group of teens who have obviously been transported from the inner city, or some institution. While desperately trying to retain an element of 'cool', they are clearly enjoying, and, perhaps, even a little overwhelmed by the spectacular nature that surrounds them. They find themselves involved in activities they would not consider as something they would be 'in to', yet, even from an outsider's perspective, you see an innocence emerging from within; a joy in being part of something much greater than themselves, and so beautifully alien to what they have been used to. It is as if who they really are arises from the person they have believed they have had to be. All just from a walk in the mountains!

And, of course, when they meet Sophie, they become the compassionate and gentle children they should always have been.

Somehow, meeting a dog allows them to let go of any pretence of being anything other than a nice person!

Love to you both once again,

Nev.

23

A Wagging Tail

Morning Nev,

Please be assured of my prayers for Kay. Her name is now written on my heart. And yes, I think you would truly enjoy Eleanor's company. She is a remarkable woman. She wrote another poem called 'Naming Dogs'. She talks about the importance of the names we give to our dogs and ends with some reflections on the name of the latest canine addition to their family:

> Tomorrow we're rescuing
> A Fox Terrier Schnauzer cross.
> Currently he's called Ralph
> Which doesn't suit him at all
> And needs to be changed.
>
> His breed has been used during conflict
> So, after Field Marshal Montgomery
> And in homage to my Dad,
> He's going to become Monty.
> Much more appropriate.

That rather typifies Eleanor's sense of humour which is, as you wrote in your last message, very English. Her naming of Monty – which I'm sure was also down to her husband Antony too (he's also a great laugh) – is testimony to that. And as for the furry scoundrel in question, well, Monty somehow broke out of his house yesterday and broke into ours. I was cooking in our tiny kitchen when he burst into the room (if you can call it that), his tail wagging (if you can call it that – it's more of a stump). He was so pleased to see me in the flesh. He's been watching me every day and night from a window across the way. I often wave to him. I must have been like a mirage in his wee eyes.

I remember when I was at vicar factory (aka theological college) a Bible translator talked about the difficulty early translators of one of the Inuit languages faced when they came to John 20:19, where Jesus, having risen from the dead, meets the disciples. John says that they were "overjoyed" when they saw the Lord. The translator who was addressing us in the college chapel reported that the particular Inuit language they were learning had no specific word for overjoyed. They looked around for the next nearest equivalent and found it in the behaviour of the Huskies. When the dogs saw their masters, they wagged their tails, like Monty. So that's where the translators started.

The disciples wagged their tails when they saw the Lord!

I can't confirm the exact details of this story, only that I remember the translator relating it, and that it's one of the few things I recall from my vicar factory days – perhaps because my Black Lab Mij and I were inseparable for those three years, and I knew exactly what message this tail wagging conveyed. But I can confirm that this kind of thing happens in translation. Mario Pei, perhaps history's finest linguist, wrote a famous book – *The Story of Language*, J. P. Lippincott Co., 1949. He mentioned that the Mexican Cuicatec language did something similar when trying to render the concept of worship. Here is the quote:

'The study of world religions is full of surprises. Just think of translating spiritual concepts from one language to another. In one West African language the world "joy" means, literally, "song in the body". In the language of the Sioux Indians there is no word for "damn" – or any other swear word. To express "Be not afraid" in one tongue of Central Africa, we would have to say, in effect, "Do not shiver in your liver." The term "prophet" amounts to "God's town crier." *And the Mexican Cuicatec language puts the concept of worship in a phrase that means "wag one's tail before God".'*

I know we can make too much of this kind of thing, especially if we have a predisposition to love dogs (also a very English trait), but the wag of a dog's tail can be very powerful, which is one reason why Sophie I'm sure had such a positive, maybe therapeutic effect on the kids you would sometimes meet on the fells. We saw a similar thing two days ago, Cherith and I. We sat outside our local pub with Bella. Two lads sat at the table next to us. Bella went and greeted one of them like a long-lost friend and then proceeded to lie at his feet for the duration! The four of us talked and laughed for ages, joined for a moment by the wag of Bella's tail! The talk was all dogs!

There is an otherworldly wisdom in all of this. We historically have tamed dogs. But they equally have tamed us. We name our dogs, but I'm sure in the equivalent of their minds, they name us too.

I love the name Sophie. From the Greek *sophia*, meaning wisdom. A dog's love is just one of the many signs of divine wisdom in the sometimes solitary and sorrowful paths we tread.

Today, in this life, we look out the window and catch a divine wave here and there.

Tomorrow, in the afterlife, we will wag our tails and meet Love in the Flesh!

Love,

Mark.

Dear Mark,

Of course, having had a succession of Black Labradors, you will know, only too well, how powerful the wag of a dog's tail can be! Sometimes, it can seem as if the whole of their back end is about to come loose: an expression of uncontainable joy. What a great picture of what it will be like for us when we come face-to-face with our Master.

One of the reasons I gave Sophie her name was because of the assumption (mainly among Collie lovers) that they have a superior intelligence to others of their species. Indeed, Sophie maintained an aloofness toward other dogs which we always found amusing. Whenever we went to a pub, she would often be sat in quiet and calm obedience as she watched other dogs embarrassing their owners with their excitable behaviour. If a dog has a disdainful look, then that was her expression. In our own pub, she was most certainly top dog. We once had a young and playful, but huge French Mastiff visit, and he wanted to play with Sophie. He was far too boisterous for her and, though he was about four times her size, she bit him on the nose – not savagely, but enough to say, "We just don't do that sort of thing in here!" He slinked off back to his owners and didn't bother her again.

One of our regulars had a dog called Orca. Orca had been brought to the pub from when he was a puppy, and he worshipped Sophie. She taught him to play ball in the pub, yet even if Sophie's ball rolled right up to his nose, he would never touch it. On occasion he would get a little over-excited and sometimes jumped up at the bar. Sophie would come along and rest her front paws on his back to calm him down. Whenever the 'biscuit man' (yours truly) came out from behind the bar with a fistful of biscuits for all the dogs in the pub, every dog knew to wait until Sophie had been given hers, before expecting to be given one for themselves.

Respect!

As you suggested in your last email, I have been pondering what name she would have given me, but I can't get beyond 'Dad'. There will be other dogs who would refer to their owners as Master, but Sophie didn't see me as her owner or even as one who had to be obeyed; she saw me as her protector, provider and friend – the one in whom she could place all of her trust.

How wonderful it is that Jesus reveals the Old Testament *I AM* is also *ABBA* – our dear Papa – in name.

If I had a tail it would be wagging.

Furiously.

Love,

Nev.

24

Foxie and Pepper

Dear Nev,

If our conversation is ever overheard, I am fairly sure we will both be accused of being romantic and sentimental, you and I, but I don't care! We are in very fine company. A few weeks ago, the day the four of us took that memorable walk together in the driving rain, we were very close to Grasmere, the town in which Dove Cottage is located. I remember the first time I visited there with Cherith being most struck by William Wordsworth's dog. There's a striking portrait of him above the fire. He was called Pepper, and the dog a gift from Sir Walter Scott. That gave me an even greater affection for the poet. I already liked him; when my dad was a POW in Burma in WW2, reciting Wordsworth – especially Tintern Abbey – kept him alive.

Wordsworth clearly loved dogs. One of his poems is simply entitled 'Fidelity.' I'm sure you know it, being the Old Man of the Fells! It's about a dog's unrelenting faithfulness to his master. The story goes like this – the master and his dog went on a walk in the fells. The master slipped from some rocks and was killed. The dog did not leave his side. Like Grey Friar's Bobby, and Japan's famous Hatchi, the dog stayed at the place, not wanting to be parted from his master, until that is a shepherd came upon the man's remains and rescued the poor creature. Wordsworth was clearly moved by the tale. He wrote:

Yes, proof was plain that, since the day
When this ill-fated traveller died,
The Dog had watched about the spot,
Or by his master's side.

Then he adds this thought:

How nourished here through such long time
He knows, who gave that love sublime;
And gave that strength of feeling, great
Above all human estimate.

Who is the "He" in the phrase "He knows"? I think it can only be God. And notice what Wordsworth says next. "He knows, who gave that love sublime . . ." As far as the poet is concerned, the love that this faithful dog showed for his master is a love that was divine; that's why Wordsworth can call it "sublime."

In the poet's mind, this dog's extraordinary fidelity was an example of great "strength of feeling." It was "above all estimate" (as in estimation). See how Wordsworth says what we have been saying: a dog's love is like God's love!

I think he gets very close here to saying that dogs have souls. In another poem about dogs – this time I think an elegy dedicated to Pepper after the dog had died – he talks with obvious feeling about the days before Pepper's death when the dog's strength is failing. His ears are deaf, his knees are feeble. He says that he saw him "stagger in the summer breeze . . . ready for the gentlest stroke of death." Then the dog dies. Wordsworth and his wife bury him at the foot of a tree, where he will forever be remembered. Wordsworth offers this tribute. He's referring to Pepper's love here:

For love, that comes wherever life and holy sense
Are given by God, in thee was most intense;
A chain of heart, a feeling of the mind,
A tender sympathy, which did thee bind
Not only to us Men, but to thy Kind:
Yea, for thy fellow brutes in thee we saw
A soul of love, love's intellectual law . . .

Pepper had "a soul of love", characterised by "a chain of heart, a feeling of the mind, a tender sympathy etc." Nev, I'm sure we are both guilty of the charge of both romanticism and sentimentalism, but I'd rather side with the poets and pay tribute to the divine beauty evident in our dogs than reduce them to an evolutionary idea – to wild creatures that have been domesticated by human beings. I'm all for being intellectual, but only if it means "love's intellectual law!" I'm all for being a rationalist, but only if the reason I'm exercising is that "holy sense" "given by God!"

So, I thought a little bit of Wordsworth would be good today – his lasting tribute to the hero of Fidelity, and to Pepper, in response to your fine tribute to Sophie.

Love,

Mark.

Dear Mark,

I made a passing reference to *Foxie* in one of our previous emails. It is *Foxie* to whom Wordsworth is referring in *Fidelity*. Extraordinary devotion – selfless, self-sacrificing, and, above all, an act of pure love. Charles Gough (Foxie's companion) fell from Striding Edge on the approach to Helvellyn; there is a plaque in honour of his and Foxie's memory further up the mountain. Just to emphasise the dangerous nature of Striding Edge, there is also a plaque at the beginning of the ridge in memory of Robert Dixon, another man who came a cropper on Striding Edge.

Many years ago, I climbed Helvellyn via Striding Edge with Chester. We had begun the walk with a friend of mine, but he froze at the start of the ridge and could go no further, so I set off along it with just Chester in tow. Had I known how precipitous the ridge was, I would not have considered taking Chester with me. As the walk became increasingly difficult, many times I had to lift him up or drop him down parts of the ridge that were too steep for him to negotiate. At one stage, I had to elicit the help of a fellow walker as I got to the top of a steep drop. Chester was just peering over and trying to sum up the courage to negotiate the way ahead. That alone would have taken some courage, but the steep drop either side of the ridge made the prospect more frightening. Chester allowed me to carry him over the edge of the drop and pass him down into the arms of the stranger who was stood at the foot of the drop. Of course, as soon as the chap put him down, Chester walked on as if nothing had phased him. I always remember the stranger's words: "My word! What a game dog!"

I am often asked what it is about the Lake District that I find so appealing. There is the obvious beauty, but it has a quality that is, in essence, romantic. William and Dorothy Wordsworth, Samuel Coleridge and Robert Southey were all drawn to this part of the world because of this essence. Coleridge explored the fells as no man had done before. He is supposed to have made the first recreational rock climb on his descent of Scafell, over the impossible rock face of Broad Stand, as he made his way to Scafell Pike, all this on his own, and with no equipment to aid him, or map and book to guide him.

The area that is now known as the Lake District was, without doubt, their muse. This ability (or gift) to be inspired to create by creation itself *is* romantic and sentimental; it is something that reaches beyond reason and intellectualism to greater depths of reality, to find, explore and, in some way, define, and appreciate beauty.

Are we not doing the very same as we consider this subject of our dogs, and what they show us of our relationship to our Father and to the world into which He has placed us? I think so. Realists and rationalists may scoff, but have they seen the beauty that we have – the beauty, the romance, of the gift of the Father that is our dogs?

Love,

Nev.

25

Argos – Not The Store

My dear Nev,

Thank you so much for that last email. I knew nothing of those historical details. Your local knowledge is second to none. But then I shouldn't expect anything less from The Old Man of the Fells! I love that we're celebrating dogs that have found their way into literature. While we're on this topic, I'd like to put in a bid for Argos, the noble hunting dog of the wandering Odysseus. Argos was loved by his master. When Odysseus was still at home, and before his twenty-year journey to Troy, the two had a close friendship. When Odysseus left, the dog was reduced to living on a dung heap. Argos clung onto life until his master returned in disguise. Odysseus couldn't acknowledge his old friend because he would have blown his cover. But the dog knew who he was:

This was Argos, whom patient-hearted Odysseus had bred before setting out for Troy, but he had never had any work out of him. In the old days he used to be taken out by the young men when they went hunting wild goats, or deer, or hares, but now that his master was gone he was lying neglected on the heaps of mule and cow dung that lay in front of the stable doors till the men should come and draw

*it away to manure the great field; and he was full of fleas.
As soon as he saw Odysseus standing there, he dropped
his ears and wagged his tail, but he could not get close
to his master . . .*

(*Odyssey* 17.313–326)

We were talking recently about the wag of a dog's tail. This,
along with the dropping of his ears (that detail from Homer is
one of the things that makes him a great writer) is very telling.
Argos had been waiting for this for a long, long time and when
the moment came, even though he was very old, emaciated, and
debilitated, even though Odysseus was in disguise, Argos could
not disguise his joy. The narrator, a few sentences later, remarks
that as Odysseus went into the palace, Argos died. It's so like the
story of Simeon in Luke's Gospel. As you'll recall, Simeon, a very
old Jewish prophet, was waiting for the coming of the Messiah.
When he saw the child Jesus, he cried,

*God, you can now release your servant;
    release me in peace as you promised.
With my own eyes I've seen your salvation;
    it's now out in the open for everyone to see:
A God-revealing light to the non-Jewish nations,
    and of glory for your people Israel.*

(Luke 2:29-32)

I love the story of Argos. It's truly remarkable when you think
that in that culture the word dog was a slur; dogs were not
generally portrayed positively in the literature of the day.

But here's the point of Argos's story. When we arrive at heaven's
gates, we will not be in disguise; we will be more radiant than
ever. And our dogs will not be lying neglected on the trash heap.

They will be glorious and upgraded versions of their former selves, and they will come bounding to greet us.

What a reunion!

Love,

Mark.

Dear Mark,

Your email turns my mind to Romans chapter 8:

> *'The created universe is waiting with eager expectation for God's sons to be revealed. It was made subject to frustration, not of its own choice but by the will of him who subjected it, yet with the hope that the universe itself is to be freed from the shackles of mortality and is to enter upon the glorious liberty of the children of God. Up to the present, as we know, the whole created universe in all its parts groans as if in the pangs of childbirth. What is more, we also, to whom the Spirit is given as the firstfruits of the harvest to come, are groaning inwardly while we look forward eagerly to our adoption, our liberation from mortality.'*

Argos is a wonderful illustration of this – 700 years before Jesus appeared on earth, Homer was prophesying biblical truth! Argos was waiting, pining, longing for his master's return. Only then could the faithful hound be happy. Only then could the dog's heart find its true home, in the long-awaited homecoming of his master.

I have always found these verses to be particularly fascinating. The Apostle Paul hints that creation has its own awareness of the end of the world's story when Jesus – our Master – will return to our planet to bring heaven to earth. The whole of creation seems to be filled with this awareness, or, at least, seems to know more than we think it does. Perhaps *knowledge* is the wrong word; creation has a *sense* of what it should be – what it will be. Is nature just waiting for us to catch on? Is that why creation is waiting for the adopted sons and daughters of God to make their appearance?

I think again of the cows in the field next door – a field which overlooks our garden. With the weather set fair today, I was able to sit outside for my devotional time this morning. I am still and quiet, deep in prayer; they are drawn to the fence, and simply stand there and watch. The obvious explanation is that they are naturally curious but, I just wonder, can they see something, sense something? Do they recognise that this is what they are waiting for?

We are both convinced of our dogs' ability to sense the spiritual. They can certainly see beyond a person's outward appearance and sense our heart, rather like their Creator in that respect. I wonder in what other ways they can see beyond. We know that some of their natural senses far exceed ours to an extent that we cannot imagine for ourselves. How is it possible to smell 10,000 times stronger than we can? Even, then, with their natural gifts they can see beyond our limits; they can even smell certain types of cancer! Perhaps, they also have an ability to perceive things in the spiritual realm that we cannot.

I love the idea that the animal kingdom is eagerly waiting for us to enter the fullness of our sonship. Perhaps we should allow them to teach us – to lead us – by paying far more attention to what the Father has deposited of Himself in them.

And now I must close. I have just heard that my sister, Kay, has been given only days to live – perhaps only hours.

I need to make the long journey south to Dorset to be with her and the family.

It may be a few days before I am able to sit down and write again.

I know that you will remember us in your prayers, so I thank you, my friend, in advance.

Love,

Nev.

26

Summerland

My Dear Nev,

I am so sorry to hear about Kay. I have been praying for her, for you, and for the family. Please do not feel in any hurry to answer this message. That can wait. You have more important matters. May the loving Father embrace and enfold you all.

I have been thinking about how to reply to your email. There is so much I want to say: I'd love to write about Homer and pre-Christian intimations of eternal truth in his writings, including how this relates to dear old Argos. I have always believed that Jesus is the incarnation in history of the longings expressed in pagan myths. When I took my English Lit finals at Cambridge, I wrote a three-hour essay on this, using Euripides. I'm like you; I believe that the stories of the ancients are often evidence of the light that enlightens every human being.

And then there's your thoughts about the cows. Do they intuit something of the divine love in you as you pray? Is their holy nosiness a sign that they are, like the rest of creation, longing for the adopted sons of God – sons like you – to make their appearance? I believe our dogs really do sense something of the spiritual realm. Our Catholic brothers and sisters argue that *The Book of Tobit* should be included in the Bible. Tobias travels with a dog. This dog seems to know that Tobias's other companion, the angel Raphael, is present. That's a positive canine portrayal – a dog that can discern angels! There have been times when I just know our Bella sees things – good and evil.

Rather than focus on these things, I think I'll conclude with another literary allusion – one that comforts at a time when perhaps you will need it most. I am referring to Richard Mattheson's book *What Dreams May Come* and his description in chapter 8 of 'Summerland' (theosophical more than theological in inspiration). I won't regurgitate the lush descriptions of this otherworldly realm, but I will pause and enjoy with you his account of Chris's reunion with his golden retriever Katie. In the film version, Robin Williams plays the lead (Chris), and for some reason Katie is a dalmatian not a retriever. Here's the source material, and some of the most moving sentences.

I started as I saw an animal running toward me; a dog, I realized. For several moments, it didn't register. Then, suddenly, it all rushed over me. "Katie!" I cried.

She ran toward me as fast as she could, making those frantic little whimpers of joy I hadn't heard in years. "Katie," I whispered. I fell to my knees, tears starting in my eyes. "Old Kate."

Abruptly, she was with me, bouncing with excitement, licking my hands. I put my arms around her. "Kate, old Kate." I could barely speak. She wriggled against me, whimpering with happiness. "Katie, is it really you?" I murmured.

I took a closer look. The last time I had seen her was in an open cage at the vet's; sedated, lying on her left side, eyes staring sightlessly, limbs twitching with convulsions they could not control. Ann and I had gone to see her when the doctor had called. We'd stood beside the cage a while, stroking her, feeling stunned and helpless. Katie had been our good companion almost sixteen years.

Now she was the Katie I remembered from the years when Ian was growing up – vibrant, full of energy, eyes bright, with that funny mouth that, open, made her look as though she were laughing.

May these beautiful words give you great hope, my friend, not only of what lies ahead for us all – especially Kay – but also of where Sophie is, and how you two will meet again – not with restraint and distance like Argos and Odysseus, but with freedom and affection like Chris and Katie. All these things await us. And by us I mean the animals too, including our dogs.

Never forget. You're a son of the Very Dear One.

All creation is waiting for your appearing!

Including the cows next door.

I'll leave you with some final lines about Summerland, with much love to you at this trying time.

Katie lay beside me, warm head on my lap, occasionally stretching, sighing with contentment. I kept stroking her head, unable to get over the pleasure of seeing her.

Mark.

Dear Mark,

These quotes from *What Dreams May Come* are extraordinary. I have read them over and over; each time with tears forming before I reach the end. Thank you for sharing them with me.

As for Kay – it seems that it is not yet her time. Over a week on from the prognosis of a few days to live, she has improved, and continues to do so. However, the few days of being together as a family, faced with the stark reality of losing one of us, has been a precious time. We have found our peace, not in the hope of healing, but in the sovereign love and will of our Father while, of course, understanding that all things are possible for Him. For now, Kay is comfortable in a hospice and, rather than continuing to circle around her, we have come home.

It occurs to me that our deliberations and considerations on the seemingly innocent question of *Do Dogs Go To Heaven?* might help to address many deep issues for those willing to consider the afterlife. Just as dogs are an amazing icebreaker and conversation starter, as we meet strangers when out on our walks, so our subject may also be a gateway to spiritual realities for many who would not normally consider such things – realities that are not just concerned with the future that is hidden from us, but also those to do with who our Father is, and who we are in Him. It may be that we catch many people unawares!

We look forward to an eternity where all our 'Katies' are restored, where the gifts of life we have enjoyed, but which have become diminished and depleted, are now fully renewed and revitalised. Love, joy, and peace will all be untainted and forever whole. It is a shame that, for so many, such things are not considered until the end of life is imminent. Yet, to dwell upon the hope of eternity is to abide in the Eternal One. It is to imagine, with divine inspiration, what life will be like when we are face-to-face with Him. It is even in that process that the veil begins to lift and we see that He is near, that the Kingdom of Heaven is upon us.

Open the eyes of our hearts, Lord.

Love,

Nev.

27

All Things New

Dear Nev

Thank you for the update about Kay and the family. As you say, our hope lies in the future when all our Kays and Katies will be restored, renewed, and revitalised (to use your inspiring verbs). As we chat about the restoration of all things at the end of time, including the restoration of animal creation, I've been remembering the first sermon I ever preached. It was in an old church in a nature reserve in Nottingham while I was at vicar factory. I was chosen by my peers to be the first 'volunteer' in my sermon class. The set reading for the evening service (Evensong) was Mark chapter 1, the temptations of Jesus in the wilderness. I chose to speak on verse 13:

> *Jesus was in the wilderness forty days, being tempted by Satan. He was with the wild animals, and angels attended him.*

I was very struck in my sermon preparation by the phrase, "He was with the wild animals." I had never noticed that before, nor had I ever heard anyone preach about it. So, with my Labrador Mij at my feet, I started to jot some notes at my desk under the title 'Jesus and the Wild Animals.' Even then, I registered the fact that Mark the Storyteller was not given to including precise narrative details, and on the very rare occasion that he did, there had to be a reason. I speculated that the animals concerned were most probably Syrian brown bears and Asian lions (both seen in the desert at the time), and that they were dangerous (the Greek word for 'wild' indicates as much).

I then reflected about the temptations (the context of this verse). In Mark's version, there seems to be an echo of the events that took place in the Garden of Eden. In Eden, Adam and Eve lived with the animals and named them. These animals were not wild because nature was still in a pristine and perfect state (at least according to the storyteller of Genesis). However, once Adam disobeyed God, the whole of the natural world – including the animal kingdom – became imperfect. The temptations by Satan were responsible for this. Even if this is more myth than history, the message is clear: Satan infiltrated the Garden. The first Adam fell. His harmonious relationship with animals was ruined. When Mark in his Gospel tells us that Jesus was tempted by Satan in the wilderness, the wilderness is the opposite of the garden; it represents nature in its fallen state. There are wild/dangerous as opposed to tame/safe animals. Above all, there is Jesus, not Adam.

What is going on here?

I think Mark the Storyteller is trying to tell us that Jesus is a kind of Second Adam, and that the wilderness is the place where paradise is about to be regained, where the curse that flowed from Eden is about to be reversed through Jesus. Satan comes to tempt Jesus because Jesus is a second Adam, but this time the second Adam resists temptation. Consequently, we see him with the wild beasts, being ministered to by angels. These wild beasts did not harm him, because he was restoring (there's that word again) all things, not just human souls.

I tried to share this several weeks later while standing in the old pulpit of the Nottingham church. My fellow students were not impressed. I think they were expecting something more practical – maybe three keys to resisting temptation. But I was not an expert in resisting temptation, nor am I today especially when it comes to fruit-and-nut chocolate bars and a good ale. But I am passionate about animals, especially dogs, and the thought of Jesus reversing the curse of the fall and giving us all a second chance to enjoy *shalom* – harmonious serenity – with even the wild animals thrilled me then even as it does now.

My fellow students of course tore my sermon apart with the ferocity of an Asian lion or a Syrian bear. My sermon class leader, Professor Tom Smail, held back from criticising me. He had a twinkle in his eye, as if he saw and loved what I was trying to say. I think he understood my love for animals. I was never without my Black Lab during those three years at vicar factory. I was known as the man with the dog. Maybe Tom was smiling because he saw that my heart was in the right place.

My first sermon was therefore about the hope of restoration. The restoration of our Kays and Katies is what keeps us going, keeps us from the despair of nihilism. I suspect that one part of Ricky Gervais's heart would probably laugh at some of what I've written because the Eden story has a talking snake – an idea that he brilliantly deconstructs in one of his stand-up performances. But I also suspect that there's a part of his heart that longs for all this to be true, so that he and his dogs don't simply fade away into nothingness (as they do in the final moments of his TV series *After Life*) but rather begin a whole new adventure in a restored, renewed, revitalised creation.

I pray that this is what awaits us.

Even as I know you do, my friend.

We keep praying.

Love,

Mark.

Dear Mark,

This is fascinating. I, too, have never noticed that phrase in Mark 1:13, possibly because Mark chapter 1 is not the go-to gospel when we are considering the temptations of Christ in the wilderness. I tend to use the Revised English Bible – a little clumsy at times, but generally truer to the ancient texts.

There the verse reads: *He was among the wild beasts; and angels attended to his needs.* To me, this evokes a picture of Jesus among a community of beasts and angels – alone, but not alone; served by angels, and with the beasts as His friends.

I understand the dangers of reading too much into a single verse but, as you say, particularly for Mark, details such as this are included for a reason. How did Jesus come to be among these beasts? They must have been drawn to Him. In the same way that creation is waiting for the sons of God to be revealed, did they, unlike the religious leaders of his day, recognise that the Son of God was being revealed to them? In the presence of Jesus, was there a restoration of the garden in the wilderness, at least in terms of relationship between Man and Beast – not just a restoration of Eden, but a foretaste of the New Creation? Did the Asian Lion lay down with the Rock Hyrax?

Then we have that word *therion* – an adjective translated 'wild', from *theria*, a noun meaning 'dangerous animal', 'fiendish beast,' 'snake' (according to *Strongs*). This got me thinking as to what form Satan took as he tempted Jesus for 40 days. Did he revert to the talking snake that had served him so well in a previous episode? Was Satan, this fiendish beast, among the rest of the community of dangerous animals that now accompanied Jesus as his friends? Was he a traitor in the midst – a sign of things to come? I wonder if the inspired piece of cinema that occurs in the opening scene of Mel Gibson's movie *The Passion of the Christ*, when Jesus stamps on the snake's head, might have occurred at the end of the 40 days in the wilderness.

In her extensive (and exhausting) study, *The Crucifixion*, Fleming Rutledge explains that the Hebrew meaning of the word *righteousness* is much more like a verb than a noun, because it refers "to the power of God to make right what has been wrong." Paul's use of *dikaiosis* – traditionally translated as *justification* – is better translated (in her opinion) as *rectification* because *rectify* – to make right – is closer to the English word righteousness than the verb to justify. I include all of that to say that the righteousness of God is *God in action*, putting right all that was lost, broken, and spoiled in the Garden.

I like the word *rectify*. It is restoring by putting things right. It speaks to me of hope that not only my own brokenness, but also the wake of devastation that my own brokenness has caused, will be, and *is being*, put right. And then, to escape my introspection, it also speaks to me of the greater hope of a broken world being rectified, humanity with it. Again, "All will be well, and all manner of thing shall be well . . ."

Is this not what we mean as we pray, "Your Kingdom come?" The advancing of the Kingdom of heaven is the rectification of our fallen world, realigning it with the eternity of a new heaven and earth existing together. My last words to Kay before I returned home were a pronouncement of that rectification to her body, as we took communion together – that *re-membering* of the broken body of Christ.

I finish with another inspired piece in *The Passion of the Christ* where Jesus, in His pain and exhaustion as He carries His cross to Golgotha – with only one eye left open and blood streaming down His face – pauses to comfort His mother and says, *"Behold, I make all things new."*

Hallelujah!

Love,

Nev.

28

When In Rome

Dear Nev,

This is just too interesting to leave! I have been doing some more thinking around what Mark meant about Jesus being among the dangerous animals of the desert. If we're talking about lions and bears, those qualify as dangerous animals. So, we are not thinking about domesticated dogs and cats here. The wild animals of the wilderness, because of the Fall, were out of sync with the original design, which was one of *shalom* – of spiritual harmony – between the human and animal worlds. However, in the presence of Jesus, the Second or Final Adam, the lion and the bear become tame because he is the Prince of Shalom. It's as if the lion becomes Aslan and the bear becomes Paddington (I can't help thinking of Paddington having tea with the Queen at the Platinum Jubilee celebrations as I write this).

On a more serious note, we know that Mark's Gospel is based predominantly on the eyewitness, oral reports of the Apostle Peter. That has a good and strong tradition to it. We need to explain why Mark's Gospel contains so many references to the sea and to boat trips. The answer is because this reflects the character and career of the original eyewitness – Peter, the fisherman of Galilee. His personality and profession are like sea fret from the ocean, wetting our faces, causing us to taste the brine and hear the surf as we read Mark's story. It cannot be a coincidence this. Peter helped Mark to tell the story of Jesus. It cries out, "I do like to be beside the sea!"

What has this got to do with the wild animals of Mark 1:13 (we are talking about lions, not fish, after all)? It's very significant. We know that the Apostle Peter died a martyr's death in Rome and that the Gospel of Mark was written to encourage Christians going through the hell of a totally unjust persecution by the most pernicious of emperors, Nero. These brave Christian souls were being led out into the Circus Maximus and exposed to the most unimaginable horrors. The Roman historian Tacitus – who had no reason to write let alone endorse Christian history, and who therefore can be regarded as a faithful historian – tells us that "dressed in wild animal's skins, they were torn to pieces by dogs, or crucified, or made into torches to be ignited after dark as substitutes for daylight." People pitied them, he says.

Now we come back to Jesus in the wilderness, among the wild animals and in the company of angels. Surely, this detail is included because of what the original readers of Mark's story were enduring. The Romans had trained their dogs to rip the bodies of these poor innocent souls to pieces – which just goes to show that the human-canine relationship is as open to misuse and abuse as any other in God's creation. To comfort his persecuted readers, Mark reports what Jesus had told Peter, that as he had resisted the devil bravely, Jesus was with dangerous animals who did not harm him (like Daniel in the lion's den), and in the presence of angels who ministered to him. To the Christians in Rome between 65-70 AD (when Mark's Gospel was published) this must have been a comfort. They were able to say, "He's walked where we walk."

Rome was the great enemy of the first Christians – the Christians of the New Testament era. They always had a terrible choice, whether to confess Caesar or Jesus as 'Lord'. In the empire, Caesar was to be venerated as *dominus et deus*, "lord and god." This is significant. Christians reserve those titles for Jesus alone. Jesus is both Lord and God. This became a matter of life and death.

I've always felt sorry for Doubting Thomas. I am not sure we've been fair on him at all. When the risen Jesus appeared to him, John in his Gospel tells us that Thomas cried "my Lord and my God!" These are the words that every Christian was asked to use in the cult of Caesar. Thomas will use them only in relation to Jesus. I'm not sure he should be called Doubting! It took courage to say what he said.

This brings me back to your idea of *rectifying* what has become wrong over time. This idea, in Paul's mind, refers to individuals, yes. We are all invited to engage in the Father's loving process of rectifying what's wrong, especially in our relationship with Him. But Paul also thinks of this process in more than a purely individual sense. The whole cosmos needs rectifying. It's all gone wrong. It's all out of alignment. Out of sync. But in Jesus, what's wrong starts to be rectified, beginning with the human soul, extending outwards towards the whole of the natural kingdom, and beyond that to the constellations. As human beings embrace the *shalom* of Jesus, they rectify what's wrong. They/we commit ourselves to being agents of transformation and restoration in every context.

This includes dogs!

The use of dogs to kill other dogs, let alone humans, is the most perverse, awful, mind-numbingly stupid idea. The stealing and trafficking of dogs – a simply disgusting trend intensified at the start of the first Covid lockdown – comes into the same category.

People who engage in such acts are perverting the original order of things, which is for human beings to brings dogs (and all animal creatures) into the loving serenity and safety of Eden.

This is how I see my relationship with Bella. In the wrong hands, Bella could become fearful and feral. But in the hands of one who is loved by the Father, she feels safe. I am with her; she is with me. And both of us are in the presence of angels. Doesn't this kind of vision elevate our relationship with our dogs?

Your relationship with Sophie was a sign of this. Such companionship/friendship is Eden restored, Paradise regained, heaven on earth.

Love and blessings,

Mark.

Dear Mark,

I, too, had thought about how it was that Peter came up with this detail of Jesus' experience in the wilderness, and why he thought it necessary for Mark to include it in his account. I like to think, that as they watched Jesus returning to them, the disciples noticed that Jesus was being followed by these wild beasts who were evidently tame in His presence. Perhaps Jesus had to be quite stern in telling them to go back into the wilderness and leave Him (for the time being). I love this thought of creation being attracted to its Creator, and I wish that it could recognise His presence more clearly in me. I believe that my dogs have recognised it, as I have recognised Him in them.

In *Christus Victor*, Gustaf Aulen quotes Martin Luther's commentary on Galatians: *"Christ, who is God's power, righteousness, blessing, grace and life, overcomes and carries away these monsters, sin, death and the curse."* This process of *rectification* that we have been considering is begun with the victorious death and resurrection of Jesus Christ – a victory over *monsters.* A monster is something that causes fear, and fear is the very opposite of *shalom.* Surely, the hallmark of this fallen world is the presence of fear. The animals fear us (and each other); we fear the 'wild beasts' both in nature and in ourselves. No accident, then, that the most common admonition in the Bible is God saying to us, *"Do not be afraid"* (usually followed by *"For I am with you"*). The monsters that have caused so much fear in this world – sin, death and the curse – are overcome and carried away in His presence. That's the beauty of Mark 1:13 – there was clearly no fear on Jesus's part, or that of the beasts. They were at peace with each other.

In dogs we find this promise of creation being at peace with us. Our hearts melt as they choose to approach us (usually with head slightly lowered, but with the olive branch of a wagging tail) wanting to be our friend. They choose to overcome their natural fear to seek friendship and the affirmation of touch and affection. I love it when a dog will run the risk of ignoring its owner's pleas of recall just to come and get some fuss from a new person who has shown the promise of friendship to them. As our friend Ricky Gervais would agree, dogs don't belong to anybody, they belong to everyone. Dogs give us a taste – a foretaste – of the rectified relationship between the animals and mankind. They are a taste of the first fruits of God's Kingdom of *shalom.*

Perhaps, the question is not so much *Do dogs go to heaven?* but rather *What do dogs reveal to us of heaven?*

I believe that the rest of creation will follow their lead (see what I did there?) in desiring to be our friend.

Love,

Nev.

29

Original Sin

Dear Nev,

I forgive you for your "lead" pun! I suppose it was bound to happen sooner or later that one of us would surrender to the temptation! Anyway, I very much enjoyed two things in your last email (besides the corny wordplay, of course). Firstly, I have thoroughly enjoyed our reflections about what Peter witnessed, knew, and passed onto the Gospel writer, Mark. I love the idea that he was struck, as we are, by the hint of the restoration of all things captured in the cameo of the wild animals tamed in the presence of the Peacemaker.

One of the first sermons Peter ever preached is recorded in Acts 3. In verse 21 he talks about "the restoration of all things." The original word used there is one found in medical literature of the restoration of full health. That's what the whole of creation is waiting for: the revelation of the sons and daughters of God and the restoration/rectification of all things. In that new heaven and earth, there will be no more monsters. None of heaven's explorers will report back, "Here be dragons!" There will be cosmic wholeness and health.

The second thing I loved was the Martin Luther reference. I think Luther gets so much right theologically speaking (although he was very misguided about the Jewish people, to the point of anti-Semitism, which was disastrous). In one of our earliest exchanges, I quoted Luther's comments about his puppy modelling to him what true prayer looks like. There's another quote about his beloved dog Tolpel. He was once asked whether his dog, and indeed animals generally, would be in heaven. His response was positive and lyrical:

"Certainly, there will be, for Peter calls that day the time of the restitution of all things. Then, as clearly said elsewhere, he will create new Tolpels with skin of gold and hair of pearls. There and then God will be all in all. No animal will eat any other. Snakes and toads and other beasts which are poisonous on account of original sin will then be not only innocuous but even pleasing and nice to play with. Why is it that we cannot believe all things will happen as the Bible says, even in this article of resurrection? Original sin is at fault."

I know Martin Luther would probably turn in his grave (he is after all the father of the Protestant Reformation), but I'm going to cite Pope Francis here – a pope named after the patron saint of animals. Early on in his papacy, he saw a golden retriever guiding a blind person. He went over to see the dog and asked permission to bless it, which he duly did. This happened in the Vatican and the Pope broke ceremonial rules to do it. It was all over the news. A papal advisor said this in response:

"We are still learning more about Pope Francis every day. [He] wants us to care for all of God's creatures. That means all human creatures regardless of faith, gender, race, culture, physical ability, immigration status, political affiliation, and sexual orientation. And of course, among God's creatures the Pope would include animals. We were given this earth to nurture, and to make it habitable for all creatures. We need to cultivate our dwelling place for all to enjoy, not exploit it."

That's a very moving summary of the theology of a man who is believed by our Catholic brothers and sisters to be the successor of St Peter – the apostle who heard about Jesus taming the wild animals, and who spoke of the restoration of all things.

And now I'm off to do a day of writing. And as I do, I won't be able to stop thinking about Tolpel with his skin of gold and hair of pearls! What wonders await us all in that monster-free zone of heaven on earth!

Love,

Mark.

Dear Mark,

That Luther quote, to which you refer, is striking: "Original sin is at fault". One could go further and say that original sin is *the* fault. What a glorious day it will be when everything is restored to how it was supposed to be before we ruined it. Whether Sophie will have skin of gold and hair of pearls, I'm not sure, but it may well seem like it when we see the things we thought we knew in the light of their untainted glory – the glory given to them as a reflection of their Maker.

The very fact that we need to ask the question, "Do dogs go to heaven?" reveals an attitude of that original sin: it's all about us. For too many, even *heaven* is all about what it will mean for *me*. The religious scoffers to such a question fall into the same trap, as if it is all and only about us. Yes, we were made as the pinnacle of creation, in God's image, to love and be loved by Him. But we were also made to care for and to steward creation, and to serve

God in nurturing that which He had lovingly made. I believe that at the restoration of all things our relationship with the new earth will be restored to that which Adam relinquished. For those of us, like St. Francis, who cherish the animals around us, it is a joyful prospect. Where I need more grace is in cherishing the humans around me just as much!

Once again, I refer to the relationship that we have had with our dogs as a foretaste of all that is to come. In the gift that has been each of our pets, we have tasted something of the relationship that we were supposed to have with all creation. I cannot comprehend it, but the restoration of all things will mean that same relationship, multiplied and extended, towards the rest of the heavenly animal kingdom.

I was thinking this morning how interesting it is that God chose to dwell with man in a garden – not a palace, nor a temple, but a garden. Father and son were together in the context of what God had created. Much of my ministry has been in worship leading – leading others into the presence of God through the singing of songs and reflecting on those songs in prayer. Yet, for myself, I find my spirit worshipping in a much deeper way when I am surrounded by the (tainted) glory of His creation. How much more, with the restoration of all things, will we worship as we see Him face-to-face in the new world all around us?

Love,

Nev.

30

Rainbow Bridge

Dear Nev,

Yes indeed. The Garden! A story, as you know, has a beginning, a middle, and an end (or so Aristotle led us to believe). The great story of the Bible has three pivotal garden scenes – one in the beginning, one in the middle, one at the end!

Act 1: The Fall of Humankind (and animal creation) in the Garden of Eden

"The LORD God planted a garden eastward in Eden, and there He put the man whom He had formed. And out of the ground the LORD God made every tree grow that is pleasant to the sight and good for food."

Genesis 2

Act 2: The Garden of Gethsemane (we should also add the Garden of the Empty Tomb)

Jesus, having prayed this prayer, left with his disciples and crossed over the brook Kidron at a place where there was a garden. He and his disciples entered it. Judas, his betrayer, knew the place because Jesus and his disciples went there often. So Judas led the way to the garden, and the Roman soldiers and police sent by the high priests and Pharisees followed.

John 18

Act 3: The Garden at the End of Time and the Leaves of the Healing Tree

Then the Angel showed me Water-of-Life River, crystal bright. It flowed from the Throne of God and the Lamb, right down the middle of the street. The Tree of Life was planted on each side of the River, producing twelve kinds of fruit, a ripe fruit each month. The leaves of the Tree are for healing the nations.

Revelation 22

Perhaps the Bible's fascination with gardens is a sign of our yearning for paradise – a word which means 'beautiful garden'. Such yearnings are "intimations of immortality" (Wordsworth). When we are children, we have a greater sense of these intimations. As Wordsworth put it, "heaven lies about us in our infancy". The Industrial Revolution deprived many of this experience, as Wordsworth knew all too well, which is why he talked about "shades of the prison house." And yet all is not lost:

To me the meanest flower that blows can give
Thoughts that do often lie too deep for tears.

What has this got to do with Sophie and Bella, Chester and Mij? We are talking about eternal mysteries here, but I'm fascinated by the non-religious version of the Christian view of heaven, especially in relation to the afterlife of the animals we have come to love in this life. You may well have heard of the Rainbow Bridge – a prose poem, which was then morphed into a poem with rhyming couplets. The meditation of heaven that these respective authors fashioned has brought comfort to millions of dog lovers over the last forty to fifty years. The Rainbow Bridge refers to a bridge to heaven located in an idyllic meadow.

In this otherworldly meadow (resembling a great garden), dogs are restored (there's that word again) to perfect health. Free from all injury and disease, they play with each other and run through the fields. The skies are always blue, the sun always high in the heavens. There is always fresh water to drink and food to eat. The dogs are happy and at peace. Except in this one regard: they miss and long for their owners whom they have left behind on this earth. What is to become of them?

When their owners die, their dogs at the Rainbow Bridge stop playing and start sniffing the air. They look towards the horizon to see their beloved owner walking towards them.

Both run towards each other.

There is joy unspeakable.

They then walk side by side as they cross the Rainbow Bridge into heaven.

Forever together.

I'm for celebrating our unique relationship with dogs.

I'm for celebrating the fact that yes, they go to heaven.

I'm for celebrating the Rainbow Bridge, or whatever next nearest equivalent lies in the great beyond.

I'm for celebrating the way the dog-human friendship opens onto the human-divine relationship.

I'm for celebrating that Nev and Sophie will be walking the Fells of the new earth.

With love,

Mark.

Dear Mark,

This morning, I woke to find out that my sister, Kay, died in the early hours. She had deteriorated rapidly from the previous night but, before that, she had enjoyed a period of relatively pain-free health, albeit in the hospice where she was cared for so expertly and with such kindness.

I think it is only with you that I can share these following thoughts. I was contemplating how I felt this morning. As soon as I heard the news, I had a great sense of her unfathomable joy – such a contrast to those dealing with her loss. My own sadness seems to be predominantly for those who are grieving, but my own sense of *loss* is something less than what I experienced in losing Sophie. Some may find that disturbing, however I am not disturbed, just interested to learn why. I cannot put this down to being prepared. In both cases, with Kay and with Sophie, I had been given plenty of opportunity to consider their deaths. I know, beyond all doubt, that Kay is in the Father's arms. Today she is with Jesus in Paradise. For me, I can say, with certainty, that death holds no sting when it comes to those who I know that love Jesus. However, Kay, like Sophie, is now absent from my life while I live out my days here. Both are lost to me for the time being, and yet I feel the loss of Sophie in a more immediate way.

As I consider this, it helps me to realise what a gift our pets are to us – what a blessing and, indeed, help. Much as my elder sister is an integral part of my life, Sophie has been a closer, more immediate, and constant companion. As I have said before, our pets – in particular, our dogs – become part of who we are. Perhaps they are given to us to provide that companionship for which our hearts cry out – a companionship we have not been able to experience through human relationship. Perhaps they are given to us to reflect the companionship of the Holy Spirit. If that is too extreme, I can think of many occasions when the Holy Spirit spoke to me through Sophie (as, indeed, He does through so much of the natural world around me).

In the end, I conclude that this is all about friendship. I loved my sister because she was my sister, but I don't think I would have called her a friend. I have a rather high bar when it comes to defining true friendship. Friends don't have to be frequent companions, but they are constant, and they are chosen. There is a heart exchange in a friendship – a voluntary binding of one life to another. That howl of grief we both experienced as we lost our dogs was a response to the tearing away of that bond. We have both discussed this before, but I say again, "greater love has no man than to lay down his life for his friend." We both know that the friendship we had with our dogs was at this ultimate level – and it was mutual.

Our deliberations and discussions of the afterlife have been healing, inspiring, and timely. It has been encouraging to consider the presence of our beloved dogs with us in eternity as so much more than mere fantasy. It has also been such an encouragement to consider our hope and our future as I have tried to support my family. It has enabled me to turn my faith into excitement for what is to come.

Love to you both,

Nev.

31

A Man's Best Friend

My dear Nev,

I am so, so sorry to hear about Kay's passing, although I am sure, as you are, that she is in that far, far better rest, as Dickens described it. And I hear what you're saying about the different intensity of response when Sophie died. I too have thought about this a lot. All through my childhood, I invested far more love in dogs than in even my two siblings, one of whom is a twin sister! As I've written and spoken about what I call the orphan heart condition, I have put this down to the fact that I was separated from my natural parent's unconditional love, that I missed and longed for that, and that the dogs I grew up with seemed to offer a reflection of that love.

I have never seen a study on this subject before, but I have often wondered if adopted and fostered children have a deeper appreciation for canine affection. Cherith works in a special school. Her headteacher takes her dog in some days – a British bulldog called Nelson. The kids love him. It's almost as if there's something about the kind of love he offers that fills a void in their hearts. But then I think, this is true of all of us, whether adopted/fostered or not. We all suffer from the orphan heart condition because we are all separated from our heavenly Father's unconditional love, at least until we come to Jesus.

And so, I am left thinking this: that there really is something about the unconditional love of our beloved dogs that shouts more loudly than a human's love ever really does of the most unconditional of loves – a love that never judges, criticizes, punishes, condemns, but simply IS; a love that just goes on being faithful even when we are faithless. It's truly remarkable. Call it friendship, yes. But friendship understood as a reflection of the friendship Jesus has with us. With their faithful love for us, our dogs remind us of what we are called to be in the presence of our master, Jesus. And his friendship with us sets the bar for the way we are meant to care for our dogs.

I think back to ten years ago when I was at my lowest, when I was alone. I knew I was sinking, so I contacted a breeder in Suffolk and broke the bank to buy a Black Labrador puppy – yes, Bella. Tiny Bella's vulnerability forced me out of my self-absorption. We lived together in a top floor flat. Every night, I would carry her downstairs – sometimes three times a night – until eventually she was completely housetrained and I, exhausted, could sleep through, with her on the floor by my side, a constant companion in the darkness.

In the morning, I would wake up and take her out. Then I would feed her. I would have a shower and she would sit by the bath watching me with her ears pricked and her head tilted. When I got out of the shower, I would start to dry myself and she would help me, licking my legs with her tiny pink tongue, her eyes hyper-focused on the task. It made me smile. She would lie at my feet while I spent the day writing. I would take her out several times, and she would try to catch the seagulls on the beach. More laughter. I would talk to fellow dog lovers, breaking the cycle of self-imposed isolation.

In the evenings, Bella would lie on my stomach while I lay on my back watching TV. She would always, at the start, try to clean my ears. She was so desperate to do something for me. I can still see her little eyes looking into mine before she drifted away into sleep. Then came the same old routine at bedtime. She would lie on the floor, wagging her little tail when she heard the opening bars of the theme tune to the USA series *The Office* – the one show that turned my melancholy into some semblance of joy. Five or six hours later, I would always cover her with my body at dawn and play with her. The thump of her tail was so hard on the floor she woke the people below.

Today, as she grows older and older, I find myself looking into her eyes and seeing things there – the gratitude yes, but also some inchoate awareness of the passing of time. I study her greying jowls, the flecks of white hair in the fur around her neck, and sigh at the first signs that her eyes are not as clear as once they were.

Even now I grieve ahead of time of what I know one day must come – a road that I have walked before – a dreadful road.

So, you are right.

It is very rare to have such a level of friendship with another human being. It is a truly transcendent thing – a hint of the divine-human love, both now and in the afterlife where Kay rests and smiles.

This human life is such a lonely walk at times. Some would say it never ceases being lonely. But walking it with a beloved dog makes it so much easier. I remember someone once saying that loneliness is not so much the state of being alone; it's not having someone (they said "someone"; I would add "or something") to share your heart with. Bella has been that to me. In the deepest pit, she and Jesus were there for me, not judging or condemning, but simply being and loving.

I would not be here today, I feel sure of this, had it not been for the love of a dog and the love of God.

Both have kept me alive.

So, yes, I understand. I do not judge you for what you have said. I applaud you. Some may be appalled, thinking that the love of a sister or a brother should be more intense and valuable. But we lose the physical presence of our siblings early on in life – in my case at the age of eight. They are not at our heels and by our feet. They are not with us in the same way by day and night, and even though we adore them too, we know that they do not expect to be loved at such a level. It's like my twin sister today. We truly love each other. But she is not at my feet right now as Bella is. She is in her home in Utah! We will text each other, but we do not enjoy the same presence.

I am praying for you, my friend, and for your family. Our long conversation about heaven seems to me to be very timely, as you say. We have both lost people very dear to us during the exchange. The timing of our intimate discussions about dogs and the afterlife seem to me to be a touch of providence in our lives.

With love,

Mark.

Dear Mark,

Your descriptions of Bella as a pup, and what she has meant to you over the years, are beautiful. There is much in them with which I can identify, and so much of the behaviour you describe would be recognisable to all who have enjoyed the privilege of raising a puppy — in particular, the post-shower licking routine and ear wash, two things that immediately distinguish the dog *lover* from the mere dog *owner*. The dog lover not only indulges the dog's desire to behave this way, but even enjoys it, whereas the indifferent owner does not.

Dogs are undoubtedly one of the clearest representations of the unconditional love of the Father that we see in His creation. As I took your email for a walk recently, I considered other ways in which they reveal something of the truth of our relationship with God.

As a Collie, as with most herding breeds, Sophie relied more on her visual sense than most other dogs. Apparently, the Collie's fascination with a ball is related to the same release of endorphins they experience when herding sheep. One of the many ball-related games she used to play with our customers involved crouching in the opening between the pool room and main bar. There she dared anyone to try to kick the ball past her. No matter how hard the ball was kicked, she would effortlessly pluck the ball out of the air before it got past her and, before you knew it, the ball had been rolled back to the feet of the kicker to try again. Many times, it was remarked that she should be in the England Cricket Team because her ability to see, anticipate, and catch the ball was quite remarkable. I read once that the visual receptors in a Collie's brain are so efficient that, to us, the ball would appear to be travelling in slow motion – hence her unbeaten record. What seemed impossible to us was relatively easy for her because of the gifts she had been given for her true purpose in life.

The same watchfulness that Sophie employed in her ball games, was also directed in a quite different way towards me. Even while concentrating intently on her games, she would always have an eye on where I was, or what I was doing. Once we had left the pub, she was no longer interested in those games. When we moved to the Eden valley, life was about our walks together, and the uninterrupted fellowship of dog and master, to such an extent that I was never allowed to be alone in a room without her – not even the loo! If ever Lesley and I had been out for a short while and had left Sophie at home, on our return, she would walk straight past Lesley to find me. Somehow, even when she was sleeping, she had a subconscious eye on me; I only had to move, and she was there, again, by my side. In her latter days, it became more difficult for her to keep getting up and moving to where I was but, with a grunt or a sigh, she continued to do so. This attentiveness towards me meant that she was able to learn and often anticipate what I was about to do, even before I had started to do it. She learned my habits, my trigger movements, and probably noticed how I went about things in ways I don't even realise, all because her priority in life was to be next to me. She would only do what she saw me doing.

It has been remarked upon many times how the attentiveness of a dog towards its master is a clear picture of how we should watch for what it is that God is saying and doing. What many have missed in this lesson is what drives that attentiveness. Why should I only want to do what the Father is doing? Because I want to be next to Him. Did Jesus disappear up the mountain to pray to receive a download of what He was to be doing that day, or was it that He just wanted to be close to His Father? It is our love that makes us attentive, watching for His trigger movements, so that we can be next to Him as He moves from room to room.

I do not envy you living in the South-East of England in this heatwave. Bella must be struggling. It is even stifling here today – a word seldom used in these parts!

Stay cool!

Love,

Nev.

32

Number One

My Dear Nev,

I hope you don't mind if we return to our beloved *Star Trek* for a moment! I know you are a fan of one the most recent iterations with Sir Patrick Stewart – *Picard*. The first season was a brilliant portrait of an old man's final, heroic adventures in his twilight years. I loved Picard in *Star Trek: The Next Generation*. When I was much younger, I didn't think it was possible for the original *Star Trek* series to have a sequel that rivalled it. But STTNG somehow managed to reach the high bar set by the characters, locations, and adventures of the original. The plaudits for that must go in large measure to Stewart, whose portrayal of Jean-Luc Picard was a masterclass.

All this is a segue into another Picard – this time Pierre le Picard, also a Frenchman. He is known as Pierre le Picard because the earliest manuscript we have of his is written in the Picard dialect. Sometime in the early 1200s, Pierre wrote a French translation of a Latin bestiary. He did this at the request of a bishop of Beauvais. A bestiary, as you probably know, is a compendium of beasts. It is a book in which animals are described in terms of their natural history. Each chapter tackles a different animal. Each chapter finishes with a moral and allegorical lesson about what the animal under scrutiny teaches us. These books were very popular in the Middle Ages.

When le Picard gets to **dogs**, he makes some very interesting comments. He starts by stating that dogs are inseparable from human beings. He says that dogs cannot live without us, the point you make about Sophie. He then qualifies the point by saying that they have three major functions as our helpers: they act as guardians of our property, as hunters of what we eat, and watchers over our sheep. He then goes on to add that a dog cures wounds by licking them, and that a young (i.e., healthy) dog cures its master's injuries. He follows this with uplifting stories about the loyalty of dogs to their masters:

- A king who was captured by his enemies but then rescued by his dogs
- A man wrongfully accused of murder who was about to be executed when his dog identified the real killer in the crowd
- A dog that refused to eat and died after his master's death
- A Roman man whose body was thrown into the Tiber and whose dog tried to keep his master's corpse afloat

After this, le Picard turns to the moral importance of dogs. He is shamelessly allegorical at this point; he says that the dog's ability to cure others by licking their wounds is a picture of the way God forgives sins wherever there is genuine confession. Of course, this is a very Catholic text in a very Catholic tradition. So, what le Picard is really saying here is that a dog is like a priest; just as a dog cures our wounds by licking them, so a priest forgives our sins by absolving them.

Le Picard goes on to say other things about dogs that are perhaps not as positive. For example, he quotes the Scripture about a dog's tendency to return to its own vomit and compares that with the way we weak human beings return to the same sins when we have confessed them. But none of this takes away the surprising and delightful thought that there are times when our dogs are much more than the natural creatures many suppose them to be; as we've said time and again, they are reminders of crucial aspects of our relationship with Jesus (our Master), and his relationship with us.

All this is to say that the way you and Sophie related to each other – a thought that you explored so powerfully in your last message – is indeed a reminder of aspects of the divine-human relationship. The seemingly endless applications of this thought in our emails to each other is one of the things that excites me most about our conversation. I never realised there was quite so much that the love of a dog can teach us about the love of God. That fills me with even more wonder!

The last few days have indeed been tough. The heat has been brutal here. I have spent my entire time for 48 hours at least trying to keep Bella cool. It can't be fun wearing a black fur coat in temperatures pushing 40. But spare a thought for humans too. My Tesco delivery man has just been and gone. I asked him if the Tesco delivery vans had air conditioning. He said no. They have cameras installed on the vans, but no AC. Imagine working in 40 degrees and having no AC. At least we could crouch beside fans with Bella. But that's just horrific. And very wrong. Tesco needs to change that situation. As Jean-Luc Picard used to say, "Make it so!"

And speaking of Picard . . . In Season 1 episode 1 of *Picard*, Jean-Luc is enjoying retirement in his French vineyard. He has a pit bull which he speaks to in French, and which lies on a mat by his bed at night! The dog's name is "Number One!"

That's just the way it should be!

Much love,

Mark.

Dear Mark,

I heard Patrick Stewart, in an interview, talking about his decision to agree to make this series. Apparently, he had made up his mind never to revisit his role as Picard, or to do anything *Star Trek* related again. However, he agreed to read the script and, of course, it persuaded him to change his decision. The second series delves into his childhood wounds (and misunderstandings) suffered in the context of growing up with an adoring mother with mental health problems, and a seemingly severe father. It is brilliantly done – with the help of the god-like 'Q'!

Your mention of Pierre le Picard's bestiary reminds me of one of my favourite books as a youngster: *A Tolkein Bestiary* by David Day. It still holds pride of place on the top shelf of my bookshelves in the lounge, next to *The Atlas of Middle Earth*. It is more than a bestiary in that it even includes an entry for Pipe Weed. However, I still remember the thrill of discovering this whole new world of Middle Earth Tolkien had created. Not just its geography, peoples, and fauna (and flora) but also its history and languages, so carefully interwoven, such that this world presented itself to the reader as a complete creation that one could so easily imagine existing in another dimension. Though it was all the product of one brilliant man's fantasy, it worked, and it was believable as an existing world.

I have just finished *What dreams May Come* by Richard Matheson, after being inspired to do so in reading your quote from *Summerland*. In contrast to Tolkien, here is an imagined world that doesn't work. It certainly has its brilliant moments, not least when Chris is reunited with his old dog, Katie. However, an imagined heaven and hell – even though they are not quite described as such definitive places — cannot make any sense without the Cross. Any attempt to imagine heaven without the salvation, transformation, and rectification of the world and humanity through the work of the Cross seems futile. Perhaps Matheson needs to take a lesson from our beloved *Star Trek* and a famous saying associated with the Borg: resistance (to the truth) is, indeed, futile.

Live long and prosper, my friend,

Nev.

33

True Desperation

Dear Nev,

You're right. We are not alone in pondering these things. Finer minds before us have explored the connection between the canine and the Christian life. The great Swiss theologian Karl Barth (famous for his Church DOGmatics) was fond of quoting a German pastor who said that God wants us to be like dogs who thrust their noses deeply into TODAY and there scent ETERNITY. Barth said that he wished that all his theological readers would become a Hound of God – DOMINI CANIS. He likened this to a monastic order, adding that he had entered it himself. I think you and I entered it four or five decades ago, although we would not have called ourselves hounds of God!

The first person to make this connection was Jesus. In Matthew's Gospel (chapter 15), Jesus is pursued by a Canaanite woman. She is a non-Jew, so the disciples ask Jesus to send her away. Jesus turns to the woman and instructs her that his priority is the lost sheep of Israel (i.e., the Jewish people). Does this put her off? Not at all. She kneels before him and begs for her miracle. Jesus tells her that he must give the bread of heaven to the children, i.e., to God's children, the Jews. She says that even the puppy dogs receive the scraps from this bread as they sniff around under the kid's table.

This is what Jesus has been waiting for – faith born from desperation; faith that is prepared to move beyond offence; faith that will persevere through any and every obstacle; faith that longs for a visitation of heaven on earth. Jesus applauds her. He tells her that this faith that she has shown has secured the miracle that she's been seeking – the healing of her sick daughter. This Canaanite woman is simply amazing. She amazed Jesus. She amazed Rembrandt. She amazed Luther. She *doggedly* pursues her Master. She kneels on all fours before Him like a dog begging for food. She tells him that she may not be one of his children but at least she's one of his puppies!

So, we are not the first to make the connection between the life we are called to live as followers of Jesus and the life that dogs live in obedience to and dependence on their masters. This connection goes right back to Jesus. Even more recently, the creators of Peanuts and Snoopy explored it in *The Gospel According to Peanuts* and *The Gospel According to Dogs*. Charles Schultz likened the little dog Snoopy (I had a toy Snoopy when I was a boy) to a mini-Christ, going around exalting the meek and tumbling the mighty!

Robert Short said "all real Christians are dogs!"

I think the reason why *What Dreams May Come* is ultimately dissatisfying is because it tries to present a route to heaven that bypasses us relating to Jesus in this life as a puppy dog relates to its master. As you so penetratingly observe, travelling to heaven without any reference to the Cross of Jesus is meaningless. No one can experience the glories of heaven, or avoid the shadowlands of hell, without – like the Canaanite woman – dogging the footsteps of Jesus, kneeling in desperation, and begging for help. We cannot be confident of enjoying heaven, let alone encountering our dogs there, unless we have learned from our dogs what Robert Short called "dependence on God" (DOG, for 'short'). We need to become desperate for God, then learn to become dependent upon Him, as a dog is upon their master.

In the days when I went around the world speaking about God's love, I always used to say that *the kingdom of heaven is for the desperate.* I stand by that. As Robert Short once remarked: "Just as dogs faithfully follow, look up to, and love their one and only master, so Christians also look up to, love, and faithfully follow theirs."

This is one of the main reasons why Tolkien is and will always be a far greater writer than so many others in our post-Christian world. Tolkien understood that the myths of dying and rising gods in the centuries before Jesus had been like divinely inspired dreams – dreams in which God prepared pre-Christian minds and hearts for the real deal, for the playing out of the same story line in history. That true, factual story is of course the story of the death and resurrection of Jesus.

Tolkien believed that we are, as storytellers, what he called "sub-creators." We create story worlds because we are made in the image of the One who created all things. This, beyond any other factor, is what makes us world builders. But Tolkien also knew that if a story is to move towards a happy resolution (what he called a *eucatastrophe*), then there had to be sacrifice – there had to be a mirroring in myth of what Jesus endured in history. That is why Gandalf must endure his death experience in *The Fellowship of the Ring*. In Peter Jackson's film version, Gandalf descends into the darkness with his arms outstretched, as if on a cross.

Because of our innate tendency to become sub-creators, uplifting stories of courageous dogs will nearly always point to more transcendent spiritual realities. Dogs are often the greatest friends we have. They are literally prepared to lay down their lives for their masters. They are, in other words, ready to demonstrate that greater love Jesus spoke about when he said, "greater love has no man than this that he lay down his life for his friends." It is this kind of love that lies at the heart of the greatest stories ever told (Samwise for Frodo, e.g.,). It is a love that inspires and transforms us when we come across it – if we are desperate – because it is a love rooted in God.

And all this comes with love – that same love.

Mark.

Dear Mark,

> *'As the deer longs for the running streams, so I long for You, my God. I thirst for God, the living God; when shall I come to appear in His presence?'*
> Psalm 42: 1-2

There is so much to chew over in your last message, but it is the idea of *desperation* that invites me to write further – desperation born out of a longing for that which we love, and for that which we depend upon. To understand that we depend on God is one thing – "the fear of God is the beginning of wisdom" (Psalm 111:10). As our bodies need water to survive, so we need Him to survive. Recognising our dependency on God is true humility; surrendering to that dependency is the antidote to sin. But the *desperation* that God is looking for is that which longs for Him, not just for the life that we receive from Him, but for His presence. This is true relationship. As Bernard of Clairveaux would have described it, it is "loving God for God's sake."

As the owner of several Labradors, you will be well acquainted with the phrase, "cupboard love". Sadly, there are many people out there whose relationship with God is something akin to this. They love what God has done for them and enjoy the blessings (and mercies) that He brings. They may even acknowledge that they depend on God for all the goodness of life and, of course, for their salvation. Yet, the Father is longing for those who are not just dependent on Him for what He gives, or even hungry for what He gives, but desperate for *who He is*. He is searching for those who are desperate to be in His presence because of the love He has for us, and we have for Him.

Now that it has been nearly five months since we lost Sophie, I have been thinking about what it is that we miss most about her. The most obvious is her constant presence. In her latter days, she would follow me around so closely that, if I wasn't careful, I could easily trip over her. She would lay on the floor right behind my feet as I did the washing up, and if I turned around too quickly, I would end up on the floor with her! Even now, five months later, I am still in the habit of watching out in case I fall over a dog who is no longer there. I am still ready with the finished yoghurt pot to allow her to lick out the remains after every meal. I still hear the sigh in her sleep at night at the foot of our bed.

Of all the things I miss the most, it is her gaze. Sophie learned to tap you with her paw if she wanted your attention – in the pub that usually meant, "throw my ball!" Often she just wanted me to see that she was there, looking at me. I would be sat in my chair reading, and there would be a nudge or a sigh. I would look up and she would be sat, expectant, gazing at me. I would respond to that gaze of love every time. How could anyone ignore that gaze? A gaze that says, "I am *desperate* for you." Sometimes it was because she was hungry, or needed to be let out, but usually she didn't want anything from me except my attention – some fuss, some play, or to be told how beautiful she was! I'm sure she understood the word *beautiful*, as she would almost become coy in response, with her ears down and her tail wagging.

Is the Father drawn to the desperate gaze of His children? I think so. The desperation that longs for His dwelling place. The desperation that loves Him with all our heart, soul, and strength. Just as I was helpless when it came to Sophie's gaze, can it be that the Father is helpless when it comes to His love for us?

For now, we only see through a glass darkly, but then we shall see Him face-to-face (1Corinthians 13:12).

In true desperation,

Nev.

34

My Master's Face

My dear Nev,

I was so struck by your comments about desperation and dependence. Isn't it interesting that the Psalmist so quickly resorts to a simile from the animal kingdom when he tries to convey the essence of what true desperation means? He likens our desperation for the presence of God to a thirsty deer in the hot landscape of Israel panting for the water in a brook. We might say, "As the faithful dog longs for their master's presence, as they search for their master's face, so we eagerly desire the Father's arms, the Father's gaze." We too would resort to animal similes. Why? Because animals are part of that general revelation in nature that points to God!

The powerful way you described Sophie's searching out of your presence, and your eyes, arrived in my inbox on the same day that my twin sister Claire sent me something she had seen on Facebook. She knows that we are corresponding to each other and asking the question "Do dogs go to heaven?" She also knows that this will inevitably involve us telling stories of being with our dogs when they die. Of all times, this is the moment when our dogs need our presence the most, when they need to see our face and look into our eyes more than at any other time in the long friendship we have with them.

And so, it was with horror and anger that I read what she sent – a plea from a vet to all dog owners not to drop their pet off at the surgery when their final moments have come, when it is time for them to be put to sleep. Can you imagine such appalling callousness? I know you and I are part of that majority for whom no obstacle would be too great for us to be there with our loved one as they pass. The vet pointed out that our dogs look for us in these heart-breaking moments before death. They search around the room for our presence, for our gaze, for our loving attention. And it is not there.

Here's what the vet (from Hillcrest Veterinary Hospital in South Africa) said:

"When you are a pet owner, it is inevitable the majority of the time that your pet will die before you do. So, if and when you have to take your pet to the vet's office for a humane and pain-free ending, I want you all to know something. You have been the centre of their world for their entire lives. They may just have been a part of yours, but all they know is that you are their family. It is a crappy decision/day/time/event every time. There is no argument against that, and it is devastating for us as humans to lose them. Do not let them transition from life to death in a room of strangers in place they don't like. The thing you people need to know that most of you don't is that *they search for you when you leave them behind.* They search every face in the place for their loved person. They don't understand why you left them when they are sick, scared, old, or dying from cancer, and they need your comfort. Don't be a coward because you think it is just too hard for *you.* Imagine what *they* feel as you leave them at their most vulnerable time and people like me are left to try our best

188

every time to comfort them, make them feel less scared, and try to explain why you couldn't just stay."

When I read that I cried with rage, as I'm sure most others did. Claire told me that it had been shared over 130,000 times. A few people had got angry and complained they didn't appreciate being told what to do. But most expressed disbelief that anyone could even contemplate not being there for their pet. Some told harrowing stories of not being able to be there because of Covid.

And I know you and I feel the same, Nev. We would move heaven and earth to be there, looking into the eyes of the one we love, as they head for paradise. Nothing would stop us.

Just as nothing will stop Jesus from being there when our time comes. His will be the last face we see when we go to sleep. And the first to greet us when we awaken.

It's all about being desperate for God's presence, for his face, as you said.

In the Hebrew language, these two thoughts are inseparable.

Panim is translated as both presence and face.

Love,

Mark.

Dear Mark,

Horror, anger, and extreme sadness were my reactions to this disturbing plea from the South African vet. I cannot believe that cowardice is the reason why most of these cases have occurred.

Rather, that the pet has outlived its usefulness to its owner; the animal no longer gives the human what he wants from his pet. In such cases, the person is only thinking in terms of disposal, and, if that is the case, it is abhorrent – a breaking of the covenant relationship we are supposed to have with our pets. The still-recent memories I have of Sophie's last moments are traumatic enough; I cannot (and do not wish to) imagine how she would have coped in those moments without me, and yet there are so many animals whose final moments are filled with fear and confusion.

I am disgusted.

The main reason I cannot think about having another dog right now is because of the memory of the pain I felt in Sophie's last moments – probably one of the worst experiences of my life. Yet, for her, I would have chosen no other way. In fact, the ways in which the vet describes the pet's behaviour in those moments, the way in which they search for us when we leave them behind, adds extra weight to what I felt the Father say to me, in consolation, soon after Sophie's death: that I was the very last thing she was aware of, the last thing she could smell and the last person she saw. It still holds such sadness, but I am also so glad that we were together at her very end.

When Chester had to be put to sleep, I was not able to be with him, as I was away in Italy for work. He lay on the sofa with Lesley and my Mum – the same sofa from which he had often pushed Lesley onto the floor, so that he could lay next to me – and he went to sleep in their arms. I hope that was enough for him, that he wasn't looking for me. Not being able to be there with him in his final moments added to my grief substantially. I determined never to let that happen again.

In her last days, my sister Karen clearly experienced that intimacy with the Father you describe so well: she looked into the eyes of the One she loved, as she got nearer to Paradise. She would often tilt her head back as she lay propped up on her pillows and close her eyes. She would explain that she was not going to sleep; she could hear all that was going on around her, but she wanted to talk with Jesus. He was immediate for her. The veil, for Karen, had become so thin that the physical world around her, and the spiritual world before her, almost merged in that hospital bed. I firmly believe He was the last person she saw here in this life, and the first she met in the next.

In our present stage of seeking out the church to which the Father is calling us, Lesley and I have had to define for ourselves what it is that we value the most in a church, and what it is that we could offer to enhance the life of a particular church family. If we have a tribe, it would be one of *Panim*. We value and honour His *presence* among us, while seeking His *face* in a life of intimacy with Him. This is all about that immediacy of relationship which is once again mirrored so clearly in our relationship we have with our dogs. One look, one nudge or wag of the tail, and we would stop whatever we are doing to give them the attention, affirmation, and love that our dogs look for in us. They watch for us, and even just catching our attention gives them joy, as we "make our face to shine upon them."

In His love,

Nev.

35

Anima(l)s

My dear Nev,

My heart goes out to you on both fronts — having to be absent through no fault of your own as Chester approached the Rainbow Bridge (as our non-religious friends would call it). There must be some to whom this applies in relation to the South African vet's poignant plea — some who simply could not be there but longed to be. And then my heart goes out to you once again in relation to Sophie's own journey from this life to the next, and you having to relive those moments. I hear you when you say that the agony of that has stopped you from looking for another dog. I understand completely. That's why it's absolutely the worst question to ask, "When are you going to get another?" You'll notice that I have never once asked you that question. Nor will I.

We have been talking a lot about the way in which our friendship with our dogs is a reflection in this physical world of the intimacy we have with our beloved Father in heaven. This is yet another reason why I simply do not understand those who say that dogs don't have souls. The word animal even contains the ancient word for soul — animus/anima. There's a clue there!

As I've been thinking more and more about this I have come to see that there are three Christian answers to the question, Do dogs have souls? Two of these are profoundly wrong. One is right.

The first I'll call the THOMIST view, commonly accepted by some of our Catholic friends. THOMIST refers to Thomas Aquinas. He had an entirely speculative view of this subject (speculative in the philosophical sense) and believed that there were three types of souls: vegetative (i.e., plants), animal, and human. The first two (plants and animals) have souls that lack intellect (or reason) and will (the power to choose). They are therefore disqualified from heaven. Only rational animals – i.e., humans – go to heaven. This view Thomas acquired almost wholly from Aristotle not from the Bible. For me, it lacks credibility because its roots lie in Hellenistic speculation not in Hebrew scripture.

The second I'll call the PLATONIC view, commonly accepted by some of our Protestant friends. PLATONIC refers obviously to PLATO. He believed that forms were expressions of a single ideal. In relation to dogs, all dogs that we encounter on this earth are expressions or 'forms' that represent the ideal of dogginess that exists in some transcendent reality. C.S. Lewis was greatly influenced by Plato; he believed that all dogs are forms of a heavenly and perfect ideal of dogginess. This means that individual dogs don't go to heaven. Their forms are absorbed into the heavenly ideal of dogginess – an idea we can reject for the same reasons that we reject the THOMIST view.

The third I'll call the WESLEYAN view, commonly accepted by those who identify with non-conformist and revivalist expressions of Christianity. John Wesley was fond of preaching from Romans chapter 8 and especially *the great deliverance* (as he called it) at the end of history. He reminded us that the whole of creation is eagerly awaiting the appearing of the adopted sons and daughters of God – those who adore their loving Father and in whose hearts the Spirit of freedom is at work, the freedom that Jesus died to give us. Wesley believed that all animals will be liberated from decay and oppression at the appearing of God's sons and daughters.

John Wesley travelled the length and breadth of Great Britain preaching this liberating message of the Father's love – calling people to get liberated from their natural condition (the sin that derives from our flesh) and from religious servitude (the fear-based and controlling religion that so often oppresses) and to embrace what he called the *filial* condition. This filial condition he regarded as true Christianity; it consists of being a loving son or daughter of a perfect Father, not an angst-ridden carnal person, let alone a fear-based religious person. This was truly a liberation theology for his day. It set people free, even as he had been set free.

Wesley travelled by horse as he preached this Gospel – 250,000 miles it has been estimated. He loved his horse and was convinced that he would meet his horse again in heaven. Not for him the THOMIST view that says that his horse had no intellect or will, and therefore no soul. Not for him the PLATONIC view that his horse was a single form representing a heavenly ideal of horsiness. These views were all too human (based in pre-Christian philosophy) and not sufficiently divine (based in God's sacred scriptures). Wesley knew that his horse – along with Chester and Sophie, Mij and Molly – will be in heaven. We can be likewise convinced and comforted.

Do dogs go to heaven? This is a tough question, I know. I guess our atheist friends will say that dogs and other animals return to the dust as we humans do, and that's the end of it. I completely respect that view. But for you and me, we identify with those non-conformist and revivalist pioneers like Wesley – and indeed Saint Francis – who believed that heaven is for animals too – and for trees, flowers, fields, and so on. In the end, I quite like what James Herriot once said (author of *It Shouldn't Happen to a Vet*): "Wherever you are going, they are going too." That leaves the whole matter open, and dependent on whether you are an atheist or a theist for the answer.

Allow me to return finally to the issue of "getting another dog" after our dogs die. I have always been baffled and a little disturbed by this question. When my oldest friend John Parkin (Sharpy) died earlier this year, no one thought of coming up to me at his amazing thanksgiving service and asking, "When are you going to get another friend?" The very idea is foolish. We recognise that our friends are unique friends, not temporary commodities. They are indispensable, not replaceable. And so, it is with dogs – a human's best friend. How stupid people are to think otherwise.

I rest my case.

Our case.

I can't tell you how helpful I have been finding this conversation.

It brings warmth to the heart as well as light to the head.

Much love,

Mark.

Dear Mark,

Your presentation of the arguments, or views, on whether animals have souls is fascinating. With unashamed bias, I have to say that the Wesleyan view carries more weight, as it is born out of a revelation of the Father and His heart for us, and for the world He has placed us in. However, I am compelled to ask, is the presence of a soul the necessary qualification for eternal life? I don't think that there is any argument whether there will be animals and plant life in the new earth – there surely must be. Our question – "Do Dogs go to Heaven?" – is, perhaps, more concerned with individual creatures from the animal kingdom, the ones we have known, befriended, and with whom we have had relationship. Of course, if we can say that animals have souls, we can then safely say that they are immortal, and our argument rests there. Sadly, we do not have such definitive evidence from scripture, though, I think, there is more than just a subtle hint!

I believe, of course, that animals do have souls, otherwise how have I had such close relationships with them? Some might say that I have projected the human characteristics of personality, character, and the ability to love and to choose onto a 'dumb' animal. Yet those accusations could only come from a person who has not enjoyed nor understood the privilege of having a pet. Yes, of course, in our love for our pets, we may exaggerate some of their human characteristics (we always used a particular voice for Sophie whenever we were interpreting her thoughts), but I am sure that we could not have such a depth of friendship with something imaginary. We have *known* the immortal natures of our dogs – in other words, their souls.

The James Herriot quote is, in my view, a profound statement as it presents another strong argument as to the presence of our dogs with us in eternity. Even if one cannot agree that our dogs have souls, there is an argument that our loving Heavenly Father would not allow such an important relationship in our lives if it were not to find its consummation in the perfection of heaven. "Wherever you are going, they are going too" is a comment that appreciates the fact that our pets are part of who we are. I have said this before, but the best way that I can explain my sense of the loss of Sophie to others is that it feels as if I have lost part of *me*. I can see no reason why my loving Father in Heaven would choose *not* to include Sophie and Chester — and for you, Mij, Molly, and Bella — in the wholeness of the life eternal that awaits us.

Yesterday, we met two dogs in a pub in Penrith, a Black Lab and a Jack Russell cross. Both competed for our attention and affection, the Black Lab winning out with the 'Labrador lean' as she sat on our feet. On leaving, I thanked the owner for letting me have my 'dog fix' for the day.

Last night I dreamt of having two puppies — you guessed it, one a Black Lab and the other a Jack Russell cross!

I woke this morning in a very good mood.

Love,

Nev.

36

Dibley's Praise

Dear Nev,

I entirely agree with you when you say that we have no need to speculate whether animals have a soul. This was really the point of my breakdown of the three views: the Thomist, Platonic, and the Wesleyan. Wesley doesn't even mention whether animals have souls. It's irrelevant to his argument. In his famous sermon, 'The General Deliverance,' he goes to Romans 8 for wisdom. There the Apostle Paul emphasizes that the whole of creation (and this includes the animal kingdom) is eagerly awaiting the "general deliverance" of all things from the decay and degeneration caused by the fall. The end of history, Wesley says, will be better than the beginning:

> "The whole brute creation will then, undoubtedly, be restored, not only to the vigour, strength, and swiftness which they had at their creation, but to a far higher degree of each than they ever enjoyed ... No rage will be found in any creature, no fierceness, no cruelty, or thirst for blood. So far from it that 'the wolf shall dwell with the lamb, the leopard shall lie down with the kid; the calf and the young lion together; and a little child shall lead them. The cow and the bear shall feed together; and the lion shall eat straw like the ox. They shall not hurt nor destroy in all my holy mountain' (Isaiah 11:6)."

Wesley's reading of Romans 8 makes it entirely unnecessary to ask whether animals have souls. His point is that when human beings enter at the end of time into the glorious freedom of the children of God, the whole of creation will experience this too. What was lost in the Garden of Eden will be restored ten thousandfold when the entire earth is renewed. Just as we – the sons and daughters of our perfect Father – will be raised to eternal life with incorruptible bodies, so will the animals and plants that we have always been called to steward and love. Our blessing will be their blessing. Their future will be our future.

It is true Wesley believed that our loving Heavenly Father has a greater love and regard for human beings over animal creatures, but he also emphasizes that the whole of creation is loved by the Father who designed and made it. Jesus says that our Father cares about every single sparrow's fate, but he adds that our Father cares about us (human beings) even more. It's therefore not either-or; it's both-and. We have an affectionate and adoring Father who loves both his human and animal creation – both Nev and Sophie.

We've been staying in Northumberland for the last week (hence my silence). My friend Tim – a former pastor just like us – told me a story about how he went for a walk along a sandy beach beneath the ramparts of Bamburgh Castle. At the time, he was going through a very difficult season, especially in his marriage. He took his beloved Springer spaniel called Dibley with him. Dibley was an extraordinary dog. Tim was told that Dibley wouldn't live much beyond his eighth year, but Dibley went on to live a very long and happy life.

Tim decided to listen to a talk given by a prophet while he was walking beside the sea with Dibley. The prophet had a mystical temperament and had been reading Mark's Gospel (chapter 16) where the Risen Jesus tells the disciples to preach the Gospel *to every creature*. The prophet started going into his back garden and preaching about Jesus *to every creature*. Some birds showed up and listened to him. Within weeks of this, all sorts of animals were sitting in a semi-circle around him, listening to him sharing the Good News that God is both his creator and theirs. The animals seemed thrilled at this.

Tim, hearing these words, was lifted out of his despair. He shouted, "Hey, Dibley!" Dibley did something he never used to do. He stopped immediately and turned his head to his master. Tim shouted, "We've got the same Creator!" Dibley then did something else he would never normally have done. He ran to Tim and jumped up at him, wagging furiously. The two embraced and rejoiced together that they both had the same Creator! Wesley would have loved that! As he said, "the generous horse" and "the faithful dog" have the same Creator and the same future as us! Sophie and Dibley will be in the new earth!

I hope this thought brings as much joy to your heart as the dogs that kept you company in the pub!

With love,

Mark.

Dear Mark,

It sounds as though the prophet was a modern-day St. Francis! I do wonder whether the rest of creation needs *us* to preach to it – Romans 8 seems to hint that creation is waiting (and groaning) for us dim-witted humans to catch up! However, I am firmly in the Wesley camp on all of this. After all, Jesus says that God so loved the *world* (*kosmos*, in Greek) that He gave His only Son.

I have been thinking over what you say about us all having the same Creator and Father; also, about how we hold a special place in His heart above all other created beings. Creation experiences God as Father in His care, nurture, and provision, but we know Him personally as *Abba,* Father. There is an intimacy with God that only we can know, even though we have been the only ones in creation to have rebelled! Creation is loved, but we are cherished.

We have a special place in God's heart above all other creatures, and yet, creation is eagerly waiting for us to realise it. The whole of creation is longing for human beings to enter the fullness of our identity as beloved sons of our Dear Father. Just as our sin has spoiled the earth and brought decay, so it seems that our redemption is essential for the renewal of all things. When we cease to perish, and start to receive eternal life, this brings everything else in nature along with us! If Sophie's eternal renewal is reliant upon me living as an adopted son of God, then I rejoice even more!

Having the same Father means that we – humans and animals – are all family. This has implications for the way in which we, as the Father's heirs, relate to the world around us. Our care, nurture, and provision for all created things should reflect our Father's love for all that He has created. As true sons, we represent our Father within creation. Perhaps another reason why creation is eagerly waiting for us to enter our sonship is that it will also mean that we will appreciate our roles as stewards of the garden – not abusers of it!

The irony, of course, is that the ones who are cherished, and who hold a special place in the Father's heart, are the ones who are the most unlovable. I'm referring to human beings – the only ones who rebelled against the Father's love, the only ones who spoilt it for every created being, the only ones who refuse to accept that God is Father of all. I rejoice in the thought that nature is my family. The challenge for me is to love those of my own species for the same reason. I celebrate animals; I tolerate humans, and I need to love them more!

This brings me back to John 3:16 again. The Apostle John often uses the word *kosmos* to represent the world order that is opposed to God's ways – humankind, in its rebellion. "God so loved those who were against Him (the *kosmos*) that He gave His only Son." If my role, as a son, is to love as my Father loves, then I still have a long way to go . . .

Lord Jesus, have mercy on me, your beloved.

Nev.

37

Our Final World

Dear Nev,

I feel as if our conversation is drawing naturally (or maybe supernaturally) towards its own ending, even as we discuss the sense of an ending in the history of the world, as revealed in Romans chapter 8. Maybe then it's time to start summarizing what we have learned in our journey together – with our invisible canine friends no doubt walking at our side. I think the main area of learning for both of us has been in veering away from arguments about whether animals have souls. I think we have both come to the point where we realize that this is a debate that owes far more to speculative philosophy than it does to the revelatory insights of the Bible.

We have both been drawn back to the beginning of the earth's story – to what T.S. Eliot described as "our first world" in Eden. Whether we read it literally or metaphorically, the truth that this origin story reveals is that the Father's intention was for human beings to live in loving *shalom* with the whole of the created world, including animals. Our divine mandate was to bring the whole of the earth into the loving embrace of the Father. It was not a mandate of control, domination, oppression. In the beginning, we were created to treat the world around us with honour, care, and above all with kindness.

When human beings decided to rebel against the Father's love, the consequences for nature were disastrous. We dragged the whole of creation with us into the death and decay that is the inevitable result of making ourselves the masters of our destiny. The whole of creation was thrown out of kilter. Everything in creation has experienced oppression ever since. Every part of our universe and planet therefore cries out for freedom from the slavery that we have caused.

But then came redemption. God so loved *the world* (the rebellious cosmos, as you rightly said in your last email) that he sent his only Son. Jesus came to put right what we had made wrong. One of the signs of that is the fact that in the wilderness, when the devil tried to tempt him as he had Adam and Eve in the Garden of Eden, Jesus spent time with the wild animals. He lived in harmony and peace (*shalom*) with even the most dangerous desert creatures. In that one single cameo, we see something of paradise regained. We see a hint of the renewal and restoration of all things through his death and resurrection. There, in the desert, Jesus is the ultimate Master of Animals!

Those of us who choose to end our rebellion and come home – like lost prodigals – into the Father's arms can now join with the restoration and renewal of all things. As adopted sons and daughters, we are called to be freedom fighters bringing liberty to fellow human beings who are the victims of injustice and to the animal kingdom (and the rest of the natural order) living in bondage to decay. Everything that knows this bondage to decay sighs with a deep longing for our appearing – for the appearance on the earth of the Father's true sons and daughters who carry the keys to freedom in their hands.

Remember the Welsh revival in 1904-5? The pit ponies were treated terribly by the miners. But when the same miners started coming home to the Father's love, when they started turning their lives around and living as God's sons and daughters, the ponies were completely disoriented. Instead of being brutalised, they experienced a revolution of kindness. It took a little while for them to get used to it, but they came to enjoy their new-found freedom. It was a taste of Eden.

So, this freedom can be enjoyed by our dogs and horses now, in this present life. But it will also be enjoyed in the world to come – in the new heaven and earth after Jesus has returned, after the dead have been raised, and after all things have been restored and renewed. In that day, among many other things, the wolf shall lie down with the lamb. Nature will no longer be red in tooth and claw. It will be restored to the harmony of Eden. Dogs like Sophie and Mij will be there, running across the vast plains of heaven, drinking from its translucent and unpolluted streams, chasing lions and tigers in the long grass, before sleeping soundly at the feet of their masters!

See how every dimension of time is implicated in this redemptive arc of the world's story. In the **present**, we start to enjoy true *shalom* with our animals once we enter the Father's embrace. This takes us (and we include our animals in this) to the very beginning of time – the **past** – when humans and animals lived in perfect security, liberty, and harmony. As we taste a little of how it was in the beginning, we then think of the eventual and ultimate **future** when all things will be renewed. Every moment of *shalom* with our animals is a foretaste of our glorious future, not just a flashback to our original past!

When Sophie died, you grieved, but not as someone without hope. You know that one day you will see her again. When Jesus returns on the last day of history, you and I will be raised with eternal, spiritual, and incorruptible bodies. We will breathe in the fresh air of the new creation. And we will see our dogs – and our loved ones – not weighed down by age and disease but liberated from all decay, running free. We will see their youth renewed like the eagle's. We will recognise them because they will be like they were before. But we will also sense something different; they will be more alive than ever!

All this makes it irrelevant whether animals have souls. The Bible tells a story; it does not indulge in speculative philosophy! And in that story, all animals are sighing – as are all trees, rivers, mountains, lakes – for the appearing of the adopted daughters and sons of a perfect Dad. Why? Because when we start welcoming that same revival spirit that John Wesley and Saint Francis inhaled, we will visit our animals with such kindness they will truly flourish, knowing in their own deep-down way that this is heaven on earth.

I don't know about you, but I want to be a character in that story.

Love,

Mark.

Dear Mark,

Yes, like you, I sense that our conversation is concluding, and all this on St. Giles's day. St. Giles is the patron saint of beggars and cripples but is depicted with a hind – a female red deer – at his feet. This is because, as a hermit, while living in a cave close to the Rhine, he saved a hind that was being attacked by hunters and suffered a mortal wound. He was a man committed to fighting injustice, both for his fellow man and for his fellow animals too. I think both of us can identify with Giles's heart.

You have summarised our conversations beautifully. We have both lost people dear to our hearts during this process and, without doubt, our conversations about what is to come – about death, resurrection, and eternity – have helped me to not only come to terms with the loss of Sophie, but to also focus my hope on the things yet unseen for us all. This whole project has been perfectly timed, as if it had been planned all along! It is such a joy to know that we are, indeed, beloved characters in this unfolding story.

Thank you, my dear friend,

Nev.

38

Rest In Peace

My Dear Nev,

I am deeply grateful to you too, my dear friend. As you say, the timing of this conversation has been providential. This has been a season for focusing on the life to come. We have both sensed it. What a caring and understanding Father we have.

I'm going to end with three separate and unconnected thoughts. When I was much younger, I used to love watching *The Twilight Zone*. I think programmes like this helped to open the dormer windows of my mind to the things that are above. There was one I remember well, about an old man and his dog called Rip.

The episode begins with the old man saying goodbye to the wife of his youth – Rachel – and going out one evening with his dog. Rip gets into trouble and falls into a river. The old man goes in after him. The next thing he knows, he is walking with Rip in broad daylight. He comes across two men digging a grave for a dog. One of the men questions why they're going to all this trouble.

"It's just a dog," he remarks.

"Not to some folks," the other says.

The old man walks up to a gate and a man appears. He is dressed as a local farmer, but he is masquerading as St Peter. The gatekeeper tells the old man to abandon his dog and enter heaven.

"That dog can't come in," he says.

The old man refuses. He replies, "Any place that's too highfalutin for Rip is too fancy for me."

The old man walks along Eternity Road with Rip. He mutters, "A dog has a right to have a man around just the same as a man's got a right to have a dog around. If needed he wants anyways to be happy." He concludes, "We'll go wherever that road takes us."

A young man meets them. He tells them he is there to lead them both to heaven. When the old man tells him what just happened with the gatekeeper, he replies, "Even the devil can't fool a dog."

The narrator of the episode concludes: "Travellers to unknown regions would be well advised to take along the family dog. He could just save you from entering the wrong gate."

That episode (Season 3, episode 19) aired in January 1962 when I was two years old. Of course, I didn't see it until I was older, but when I did watch it, it made a deep impression. It's a beautiful story, full of deeper meaning too. At first, I thought the dog's name was strange ("Rip"), until I realised that it was a play on words – R.I.P. Rest in Peace! In fact, you could say that the whole episode is a short meditation on the title of this book, *Do Dogs Go to Heaven?* The answer is clearly yes. Indeed, the message is this: no dog lover could ever truly rest in peace unless they have their beloved canine friend with them along Eternity Road. What a blessed thought that is!

I think both of us would agree with the young man at the end (clearly a wingless angel). To live without your dog in eternity would be hell indeed. And for heaven to be truly heavenly, we will all need to walk into its fields with our animals by our side.

The Rips of this world are waiting for us, my friend.

Doesn't that warm the soul?

Much love,

Mark.

Dear Mark,

This is great! The young man sounds like Jesus to me: *"I am here to lead you both to heaven"*. In the dog's acceptance of the young man, it has ensured that both he and his master have entered through the right 'gate'.

This *Twilight Zone* episode rather sums up what we have both been discussing; how Jesus' redemption is for the world and not just for humanity. He is here to lead us *both* to heaven.

Also, in his comment, "Even the devil can't fool a dog" we see something of what we have been discussing in relation to how our pets can reveal so much about the relationship we have with our Heavenly Father.

Whoever wrote the story for that episode was undoubtedly inspired.

Love,

Nev.

39

Beautiful Joe

My Dear Nev,

My next "final" thought is shorter. It is a quotation from the end of a novel that was immensely popular and successful in its day – *Beautiful Joe. A Dog's Story*. It's the story – told by the dog himself – of a dog's life and death. It was based on the true and traumatic story of a dog rescued by someone the Canadian author, Margaret Marshall Saunders, knew. It was published in 1893 and by the turn of the century had sold 800,000 copies in America. It was the first Canadian book to sell over one million copies. The sequel, *Beautiful Joe's Paradise*, is said to have been part of the inspiration for the idea of the Rainbow Bridge which we discussed earlier in our conversation.

I won't ruin the novel by telling you the story of *Beautiful Joe*. I'll just quote what the beloved dog says to the reader at the end. It's written in the idiom and style of its day, so there's perhaps an overly moralistic tone, and there's also a reference to "dumb animals" that's similarly dated. But the message Joe (the dog) has left us with in the final sentences of his story is timeless.

"Now, I must really close my story. Goodbye to boys and girls who may read it; and if it is not wrong for a dog to say it, I should like to add, 'God bless you all.' If in my feeble way I have been able to impress you with the fact that dogs and many other animals love their masters and mistresses, and live only to please them, my little story will not be written in vain. My last words are, 'Boys and girls, be kind to dumb animals, not only because you will lose nothing by it, but because you ought to; for they were placed on the earth by the same Kind Hand that made all living creatures'."

May you and I, and our loved ones (including especially our dogs), be blessed by God's Kind Hand.

As the Good Book says,

> The godly care for their animals,
>   but the wicked are always cruel.

Proverbs 12:10

Dear Mark,

Two wonderful stories, there, to finish. I eagerly anticipate your final offering! We are clearly not alone in our thinking, in our affection for our dogs, and our desire to have them by our side forever.

I have recently experienced a touch of heaven at the Patterdale Dog Day – The Ullswater Sheep Dog Trials – a day surrounded by Collies and Labradors, and a place where everyone was happy to talk about their dogs and share the love.

It is a beautiful thing to be greeted by a dog as if you were a long-lost friend, even though it has never met you before. For a few minutes of fuss and cuddles, each one was, indeed, my friend.

I'm really not sure how much longer I can go without finding another one of my own.

Love,

Nev.

40

An Enchanted Place

Dear Nev,

That last sentence has me intrigued and excited in equal measure! I cannot wait to see what happens next!

Nev, we began this very long correspondence (as it has turned out, unexpectedly to both of us) with mourning Sophie, and in many ways our wide-ranging discussion has been as much about grief as it has been about our beloved canine friends, and of course other animals too. My prayer has always been that the Father would comfort you, giving you blessed memories of your past with Sophie, while also consoling you that the best with her is yet to be.

When it comes to grief over our animals, my soul is drawn to what is perhaps an unexpected place. I am referring to the very end of the Winnie the Pooh stories where it is time for Christopher Robin to move on from his childhood days – days of "doing Nothing" with his talking animal friends. It is an incredibly poignant and poetic piece of writing. Many have been lastingly touched by it, and still – well into their adult years – shed a tear even at its mention.

So, what's all the fuss about?

After Christopher Robin has said goodbye to the other animals, he invites Pooh out for one final walk to an "enchanted place" –

a place where over sixty trees have grown in a circle. On the way, the boy asks Pooh a question:

> *Christopher Robin, who was still looking at the world, with his chin in his hand, called out "Pooh!"*
> *"Yes?" said Pooh.*
> *"When I'm – when – Pooh!"*
> *"Yes, Christopher Robin?"*
> *"I'm not going to do Nothing anymore."*
> *"Never again?"*
> *"Well, not so much. They don't let you."*
> *Pooh waited for him to go on, but he was silent again.*
> *"Yes, Christopher Robin?" said Pooh helpfully.*
> *"Pooh, when I'm – you know – when I'm not doing Nothing, will you come up here sometimes?"*
> *"Just me?"*
> *"Yes, Pooh."*
> *"Will you be here too?"*
> *"Yes Pooh, I will be really. I promise I will be Pooh."*
> *"That's good," said Pooh.*
> *"Pooh, promise you won't forget about me, ever. Not even when I'm a hundred."*
> *Pooh thought for a little. "How old shall I be then?"*
> *"Ninety-nine."*
> *Pooh nodded. "I promise," he said.*
> *Still with his eyes on the world Christopher Robin put out a hand and felt Pooh's paw.*

I think it's here, in this unforgettably touching scene, that we get to the heart of A.A. Milne's thoughts. Christopher Robin has spent his life thus far "doing Nothing." Now there's being idle – when you should be working – and there's being a child, when you should be doing Nothing, nothing except being so filled with wonder at even the smallest things that time seems to stand still, or not exist at all. The boy has come to the end of this phase of his life. It's time to move on.

I don't want to think about what Christopher Robin is heading towards. I'd like to finish our correspondence with a few thoughts about where he's been. Here, in an enchanted place at the top of the forest, Christopher Robin steps away from a season of his life where he has simply enjoyed doing Nothing with his animal friends. Doing Nothing hasn't meant being passive. They have had had many adventures, after all. It means finding everything wonderful!

I think heaven will be like this. Obviously – before the piety police set off their lamentable sirens – heaven will be primarily where we are lost in wonder, love, and praise over the matchless majesty of the One who loves us like no earthly father – even the best – ever has. But I suspect it will also be the realm in which we do Nothing in the rich, deep-down, lush sense in which Milne meant it, that pristine, innocent, immersive consciousness we enjoyed with the animals in Eden.

I think many of us lose that sense of awe, curiosity, and adventure when we grow up and are no longer either allowed to do Nothing or too busy to engage in this childlike state. But I suspect that when we play with our dogs, when we talk with them, when we walk and run with them, we are re-enacting just for a few fleeting seconds that primal enchantment of Eden, and of childhood, when doing Nothing was more than okay, and where play and exploration were our normal.

And here's how Milne ends it all, in one of the most beautifully written paragraphs ever penned.

"So, they went off together. But wherever they go, and whatever happens to them on the way, in that enchanted place on the top of the Forest, a little boy and his Bear will always be playing."

"That enchanted place on the top of the Forest..."

What a perfect phrase that is!

The place where the boy and his animals talked and played.

That's heaven.

Being childlike again.

Where doing Nothing is everything.

In the presence of God.

Reunited with our animals.

With Sophie.

With Mij.

With Chester.

With Molly.

In an enchanted place.

Thank you for everything you have shared in our conversation, my friend. It has been so enriching.

With fond love,

Mark.

Dear Mark,

This is a perfect ending. This *doing Nothing* in, as you say, "the primal enchantment of Eden" is exactly where I have been for the last two and a half years — actually, quite literally in Eden, as we live in the beautiful Eden valley. Since my spiritual awakening at Toronto in the mid 90's, I have lived with the understanding that Jesus said there is "only one thing necessary" (Luke 10:42), something with which so many religious types would take issue, because that one thing necessary could so easily be misunderstood as inactivity and passivity. When we first moved here, I heard the Holy Spirit say that I was here for purity, creativity, and rest. In this almost monastic existence, I have enjoyed being graced with all three to the place where I am now ready to return to the world and ministry among people, rather than sheep and cows. It has been a time of transformation and equipping, of adventure but also of sorrow. Above all, it has been a time of reflection.

This conversation has magnified, intensified, and focussed that reflection in the most profound and valuable way. As you say, what a wonderful and caring Father we have.

Christopher Robin says that he is no longer going to be able to "do Nothing" because "*they* don't let you."

It's a lie, Christopher!

With much love and gratitude for all that you have poured out over this *conversation.*

Nev.